W9-CLG-968

Frank Norris Revisited

Twayne's United States Authors Series

Nancy Walker, Editor
Vanderbilt University

TUSAS 610

Frank Norris
From the Collection of Joseph R. McElrath, Jr.

Frank Norris Revisited

Joseph R. McElrath, Jr.

Florida State University

Twayne Publishers ∎ New York

Maxwell Macmillan Canada ∎ Toronto

Maxwell Macmillan International ∎ New York Oxford Singapore Sydney

Frank Norris Revisited
Joseph R. McElrath, Jr.

Copyright 1992 by Twayne Publishers

Twayne Publishers   Maxwell Macmillan Canada, Inc.
Macmillan Publishing Company   1200 Eglinton Avenue East
866 Third Avenue   Suite 200
New York, New York 10022   Don Mills, Ontario M3C 3N1

Macmillan Publishing Company is part of the Maxwell Communications
Group of Companies.

Library of Congress Cataloging-in-Publication Data

McElrath, Joseph R.
    Frank Norris revisited / Joseph R. McElrath, Jr.
        p. cm. – (Twayne's United States authors series; TUSAS 610)
    Includes bibliographical references and index.
    ISBN 0-8057-3965-3 (alk. paper)
    1. Norris, Frank, 1870-1902 – Criticism and interpretation. I. Title.
II. Series.
PS2473.M34   1992
813'.4 – dc20   92-4769
                                                        CIP

The paper used in this publication meets the minimum requirements of
American National Standard for Information Sciences – Permanence of
Paper for Printed Library Materials, ANSI Z39.48-1984.

10 9 8 7 6 5 4 3 2 1

Printed in the United States of America.

For

Joseph R. McElrath

and

Marguerite Hodges McElrath

Contents

Preface

Frank Norris Revisited is the sequel to one of the most influential introductions to the life and works of Norris, Warren French's *Frank Norris* of 1962. When French's study appeared, Frank Norris was still in eclipse. Since 1903, when *The Pit* was the year's best-selling novel and widely hailed as "the Great American Novel," Norris's reputation had declined. He remained a significant figure in literary histories by virtue of his early contributions to the sensational Naturalistic novel tradition initiated in the 1890s. He had clearly extended the gains in frankness and intellectual freedom won by the Realists and particularly their spokesman, William Dean Howells. But Norris was hardly a household name a half-century later.

French changed that with his lively, provocative study by not only placing Norris in the popular culture of his time and ours but arguing that Norris was a scion of the American Transcendentalists, having much in common with such well-known figures as Henry Thoreau and Ralph Waldo Emerson. Norris's stock immediately increased in value. Donald Pizer's *The Novels of Frank Norris* appeared in 1966; William B. Dillingham's *Frank Norris: Instinct and Art* was published in 1969. In the 1970s, other books and an increasing number of articles began appearing. A renaissance had occurred.

Since 1962, Norris scholarship has become a particularly vital area of not only literary research but cultural study, with Frank Norris as the touchstone for turn-of-the-century changes in art and thought. Much more biographical data have been unearthed and analyzed; a plethora of interpretive approaches to the Norris canon has materialized.

This volume seeks not to "update" Warren French's introduction to Norris. French's work now has an identity and an integrity with which no one should tamper. Rather, the intent is to provide an independent and complementary portrait of the artist. French and I do not always agree on either what Norris intended or what he actually accomplished. The truth probably lies somewhere between the two introductions now available, although I of course have my own opinion as to which version of the historical reconstruction is preferable. As French said to me at the time he suggested I undertake this project, let the best man win, but let neither assume that a "definitive" profile of the elusive Norris is possible. Given the dearth of biographical information that still faces the scholar, despite the progress made in the last 30 years, I can only second his caveat.

Chronology

1870	Benjamin Franklin Norris, Jr., born 5 March in Chicago.
1878	Family tours Europe.
1884	Family moves to Lake Merritt in Oakland, California.
1885	Family moves to San Francisco. Norris attends a private academy in Belmont, south of San Francisco.
1886	Norris studies drawing and painting at the San Francisco Art Association.
1887	Family accompanies Norris to Paris, where he studies art at the Académie Julian. Develops an interest in opera and medieval culture and sends chivalric tales to his brother, Charles (b. 1881).
1889	Composes a now-lost prose fiction, "Robert d'Artois." His first publication, the newspaper article "Clothes of Steel," appears.
1890	Enters the University of California, continues writing, performs in theatricals, and becomes an active member of Phi Gamma Delta fraternity.
1891	Writes poetry and short stories. *Yvernelle* published in December.
1892	Father separates from family.
1894	Parents divorce. Norris leaves the University of California without a degree. Studies French literature and writing at Harvard University.
1895	Leaves Harvard, having written compositions closely related to *McTeague* and *Vandover and the Brute*. Continues to publish in West Coast periodicals.

1896	Arrives in South Africa, writes travel essays, and becomes involved in the Jameson Raid. Returns to San Francisco and begins two-year tenure as writer and editorial assistant for *The Wave*.
1897	Completes *McTeague* manuscript at the Big Dipper Mine near Colfax, California.
1898	*Moran of the Lady Letty* is serialized in *The Wave*. Norris works as a journalist for the S. S. McClure syndicate in New York City, covering the Spanish-American War from Cuba. *Moran* published. Norris begins *Blix* in San Francisco.
1899	*McTeague* published. *Blix* is serialized, revised, and published. *A Man's Woman* is written and serialized. Norris conceives "The Epic of the Wheat" trilogy and begins research on *The Octopus*.
1900	Leaves S. S. McClure when Doubleday & McClure Co. dissolves; works as manuscript reader for Doubleday, Page & Co. Marries Jeannette Black in New York City 12 February. *A Man's Woman* published. Norris writes *The Octopus*.
1901	*The Octopus* published. In Chicago Norris begins research on *The Pit*. Resumes writing literary essays and short stories. Writes *The Pit* in New York City.
1902	Continues writing short stories and essays as well as *The Pit*. Daughter, Jeannette, born 9 February; family moves to San Francisco in July. Norris makes preliminary plans for research on *The Wolf*. An abbreviated version of *The Pit* is serialized beginning in September. Norris envisions writing a trilogy on the Battle of Gettysburg. Dies 25 October of peritonitis following an appendectomy.
1903	*The Pit* published. Norris's brother, Charles, arranges for publication of short story (*A Deal in Wheat*) and literary essay (*The Responsibilities of the Novelist*) collections. *Complete Works* (7 vols.) appears.

1909   *The Third Circle*, a collection of short stories, pub-
            lished.

1914   *Vandover and the Brute*, edited by Charles G. Norris,
            published.

Chapter One

A Novelist in the Making

Norris's Achievement

When Benjamin Franklin Norris, Jr., died at age 32 on 25 October 1902, he was known as one of the most prolific and promising novelists of his generation. Yet, while he had achieved fame in America and England by that time, Frank was hardly a boy wonder. His first novel, *Moran of the Lady Letty*, did not appear until September 1898, when he was 28, after approximately 200 shorter writings (short stories, poems, literary and "local color" essays, sports reports, interviews with artists, and book and play reviews) appeared in California periodicals. Through 1897, his reputation as a short-story writer and essayist was modest and limited to the environs of San Francisco. But once he had broken into the world of East Coast publishing, he made rapid progress.

Moran was followed in fewer than six months by the work now judged his masterpiece, *McTeague* (1899). Only seven months later appeared *Blix* (1899). The reviewers were amazed by the productivity of the newcomer on the national scene.[1] Furthermore, the extraordinary versatility displayed within 13 months was remarkable: rare is the writer making his debut by producing three novels so unlike each other. The luridly thrilling episodes of *Moran* were sensationally fashioned along the lines of adventure-romances such as those for which Robert Louis Stevenson was famous. *McTeague* was quite different: it stood as the first full-scale American example of the Naturalistic novel that Emile Zola was producing in France. Like Zola's sensationally graphic study of degeneracy, *L'Assommoir* (1877), *McTeague* startled and offended polite Americans with its frank, post-Darwinian portrait of human nature and its representations of sexual arousal, brutal violence, and psychopathology in lower-middle-class and slum environments. *Blix* next took the reader

1

to the opposite extreme in the realm of taste, where the upper middle-class characters and settings are a good deal nicer. It was in the vein of Richard Harding Davis's disarmingly pleasant love idylls featuring good young people who triumph over adversities to know happiness. Dedicated to Norris's mother, *Blix* was as optimistic and "clean" as *McTeague* was pessimistic and "dirty." What would Norris try next?

A Man's Woman (1900) was published only four months after *Blix*, as Norris kept up his breakneck pace. His best-seller to this point was also a novelty: a psychological study of the gargantuan egotism of two would-be lovers. Fourteen months later *The Octopus* (1901) was published. It was an infinitely better work than the bizarrely overwrought melodrama that preceded it. With *The Octopus*, his most massive and complex novel, Norris appeared to rise to the status of a world-class author, offering a full-scope analysis of American life and values as represented in the economic arena of fin de siècle California.

Then, suddenly, the career was over. While an abbreviated version of the second volume of his ambitious "Epic of the Wheat" trilogy was being serialized in the *Saturday Evening Post* in late 1902, Norris was struck down by peritonitis following an appendectomy. In the mind of his generation, *The Pit* (1903) was his masterwork. This domestic tragicomedy, framed by an exposé of speculation at the Chicago Board of Trade and featuring another close study of egotism, was for months the best-selling novel in America. It was praised by many as, at last, *the* Great American Novel.

In only four years, then, Norris earned an eminent place in the literary world. A collection of literary essays, *The Responsibilities of the Novelist*, and another of short stories, *A Deal in Wheat*, quickly followed *The Pit* in 1903 – as did the seven-volume *Complete Works*, commemorating Norris's most substantial writing achievements. His seventh novel, *Vandover and the Brute*, was posthumously published in 1914. Today Norris is a touchstone figure in American literary histories, representing the school of Literary Naturalism. For intellectual historians he is important as well: like Stephen Crane, Henry Adams, and Kate Chopin, Norris registered dramatically the transition from the age of Emerson, Thoreau, and Whitman to that of Fitzgerald and Steinbeck. More specifically, he signalled the movement away from Victorian cultural values – and especially from the defunct metaphysical idealism that Zola so despised – to the more positivistic and pragmatic modern sensibility at the turn of the century. As such he provides an important example of what it meant to be both post-Victorian and pre-Modernist in the fashion of other Progressive Era writers and thinkers with humanistic interests and humane values.

Art and Life

Developing an understanding of Norris's life is difficult. Having died young without writing any memoirs and having burned the correspondence between his wife and himself, Frank Norris in addition deprived biographers of information by refraining from commenting directly upon his life in other than the most perfunctory way. Notebooks, diaries, letters, and other biographically significant documents preserved by Norris's mother were destroyed during the 1906 San Francisco earthquake. Other family members were quite careless about additional materials that survived the earthquake. In short, relatively little primary data concerning Norris's life is available. What is first inferable, however, is that while others have suffered worse than he, Norris was profoundly affected by a disquieting home environment. The maturation topic central to his novels relates not only to Frank's experience of his own protracted adolescence but also to the disruptive behavior of his apparently immature parents. Both behaved like children as they reared their children.

The melancholic teenager recalled by his uncle, W. A. Doggett, was born on 5 March 1870 in Chicago, where he lived until he was 14. Extremely little is known about Norris's earliest years beyond what was suggested by his fiction and confirmed after his death by his younger brother, Charles G. Norris (1881-1945).[2] His last novel, *The Pit*, for example, has long been recognized as autobiographical and was commented on as such by Charles. Set in Chicago's upper-middle-class society, it focuses on the sumptuous kind of life that was the Norrises' during the Gilded Age. There are no children in that novel, though, and the most personal dimensions of Norris's experience the novel reveals relate to his mother's and father's incompatible personalities and the tensions in their relationship.

The heroine of *The Pit*, Laura, is a would-be actress given to egocentricity, who neurotically requires virtual adoration from an increasingly neglectful husband whose romantic ardor has markedly cooled three years after the wedding. That Frank was born three years after his parents' marriage thus seems significant: the novel's chronology suggests that Norris's recollection was of a family already in crisis during his earliest years. All that we know about Norris's histrionic mother, the one-time Shakespearean actress Gertrude G. Doggett (1840-1919), squares with the attractive and unattractive traits that Norris assigned to Laura, especially her virtual mania for being the center of attention. Likewise, the previously married B. F. Norris (1836-1900) was in many ways the cloth from which the hero of the novel, Curtis Jadwin, was cut. Like Curtis, he was a driven entrepreneur and did not share Gertrude's fervid enthusiasm for things aesthetic. He was a down-to-earth Michigan farm boy (again like Curtis) who came to the big city to reap wealth from jewelry sales. Financially and socially, B.F. had "arrived" by 1867 when he won Gertrude away from the stage. His victory, however, proved a Pyrrhic one: the unsatisfying marriage reached its terminus by 1892 at the latest. B.F. then had had enough and left the family to take an extended pleasure trip. Gertrude had refused to accompany him, and B.F., accustomed to winning at the high-stakes games he played in the American marketplace, was as predisposed to having his way as Gertrude. Furthermore, Norris family lore has it that B.F. truly behaved like a "brute," as Victorian Americans would have put it. He made his trip with another woman, and Gertrude angrily initiated divorce proceedings in 1894. Gertrude went public, charging deser-tion; B.F. told journalists that she deserted *him* – his rationalization being, apparently, that her refusal to travel was a passive act of abandonment. It was not an amicable separation to say the least, though Gertrude received a generous settlement. In a final act of vindictiveness and self-pity, she listed herself in the city directory as "widow." Like Laura, Gertrude inclined toward grand gestures in the limelight.

Charles Norris's correspondence and his interviews with Frank's biographer, Franklin Walker,[3] in the 1930s confirm two facets of Frank's early life suggested by *The Pit*. First, he passed his childhood and entered adolescence in regal surroundings: he had servants, car-riages, a pet pony, and other amenities of the leisure class, including a year at the prestigious Harvard School with other privileged youths just before the family moved from Chicago to California in 1884. Second, life in this family became increasingly stressful. The death in 1869 of a three-month-old daughter, Grace, perhaps complicated matters. Her birth certainly had, because it prevented Gertrude from pursuing the theatrical career B.F. had promised she could continue. Gertrude never got over this betrayal, convinced that B.F. had privately planned that she would never return to the theater. Another daughter, Florence, was born two years after Frank; the death of this one-year-old in 1873 was an additional strain, to be felt again in 1887 when 11-year-old Lester died.

B.F. had reasons to be "considerate" to Gertrude, as Charles said he *once* was. But patience with a wife – whose extreme self-absorption seen in Charles's correspondence years later must have manifested itself much earlier – had its limits. The merchant prince and the self-styled grande dame given to performing off-stage eventually had little in common other than the vicissitudes through which they had passed. Furthermore, B.F. had needs that Gertrude did not satisfy. Like Curtis in *The Pit*, he looked outside the family for gratification.

When and to what extent B.F. became a philanderer is not certain. Again, Norris did not directly comment on his early years. But that problems of this kind affected him by the time B.F. took his world cruise, possibly with a woman named Belle who became his third wife, is a means of interpreting one of Norris's earliest short stories. "The Way of the World" can be read against a biographical background in which Gertrude was devoting her energies to San Francisco's Browning Society, she being that group's prima donna of elocution and generally a very visible, and audible, member of the city's "high society." Meanwhile, B.F. was tending to his jewelry firm in Chicago and real estate ventures in San Francisco, and perhaps showing a special kind of interest in the theater. "The Way of the World" is the story of a young man who amateurishly seeks the attention of an actress of dubious virtue. He discovers at length that he has a rival. Entering her dressing room one evening, he is more than a little surprised to find his father there. The story was published in the San Francisco *Wave* in 1892, the year B.F. deserted not only Gertrude but also his sons.[4]

One would not want to push autobiographical interpretation too far, picturing Norris discovering his father in the throes of illicit passion. For one thing, the tone of the story is not "tragic" – although Norris would not be the first artist to distance himself from unpleasant personal experience by means of a "light" fictional treatment. What Frank *had* witnessed in his father's betrayal, however, appears to have determined his portrayals of relations between the heroes and heroines of his later fiction: he never executed a full-scale picture of a successful, long-term marriage; on the other hand, he repeatedly produced novels analyzing the complex dynamics of male-female relationships. It is one of the constants in his canon. How does one create and maintain a truly positive bond with a member of the opposite sex? In his private life, the question and its answer were also paramount: he appears to have worked very hard at ensuring the success of his 1900 marriage to Jeannette Black; they were inseparable and, to a significant degree, coworkers. Friends credited her with having contributed much to Norris's writing. Like Charles with Kathleen Thompson Norris, who in fact saw Frank and Jeannette's marriage as their model, Norris was determined to succeed where his parents had so dramatically failed.

A Question of Masculinity in the Mauve Decade

By the time he was in his twenties, Frank Norris appeared to be one of San Francisco's "gilded youths," carelessly larking about with other well-heeled young society men. The overgrown, well-to-do college boy described by Franklin Walker was, to a large degree, the very image of the glittering young swells then being described as carefree bons vivants by the enormously popular Richard Harding Davis and so attractively drawn by Charles Dana Gibson. But unlike Davis's men-about-town, Frank had faced, and was still facing, difficulties unknown to those fictional figures.

For example, philandering aside, there were other tensions in his relationship with B. F. Norris. For many years Frank could not be termed "his father's son," in the sense of the vigorous, aggressive male image his father projected. Like the hero passing through adolescence in *Vandover and the Brute*, the young man who moved to the West Coast from Chicago in 1884 was tall, thin, and suffered facial blemishes. When he was sent to a private school in Belmont, south of San Francisco, his single known attempt at athletic prowess resulted in a broken arm and an end to football playing. He later tried fencing, but for an American male that was hardly the same thing as football. Indeed, it seems a sport more to Gertrude's liking, given her Romantic flair and habit of reading to her sons from the chivalric romances of Sir Walter Scott. The pattern traceable in the early California years strongly suggests that, like Charles, Frank had early fallen under the dominating influence of his mother. B.F. wrote the checks and sharply observed the yield from his investments, while Gertrude devoted herself to molding character – specifically, the personality of an artist. Charles, too, would become a novelist.

The Making of an Artiste

Gertrude's assertively guiding hand and Frank's compliance are especially apparent in the decisive step taken in his progress toward a career as an artist rather than a businessman. Living at home again, Frank was enrolled by 1886 at San Francisco's Art Association school under the direction of a painter today appreciated for his excellence in still-life work, Emil Carlsen. How much he enjoyed this is not clear; much later he would make sarcastic references to the hours spent by art students in drawing onions and stone jugs.[5] But he persisted in developing his flair, and in 1887 his father was escorting him to Europe. Gertrude remained at home with the fatally ill Lester.

Lester had been the fair-haired son in Gertrude's eyes. On his death Frank became the doted-on child, while Charles suffered the neglect that glosses the acute sensitivities to friendship, love, and family life displayed in his writings. Lester interred, Gertrude and Charles joined B.F. and Frank, and the family settled for the while in London. Frank studied at the art school at the South Kensington Museum: the onions and stone jugs were replaced by the many plaster molds of major continental art works in its enormous collection. Then in late 1887 it was on to Paris, where Frank entered the Académie Julian and studied with one of the masters of Academic painting, Guillaume Bouguereau, under whose tutelage he learned more about the conventions of mainstream high art of the Romantic-Victorian order. The orthodox idealistic tastes of the mother devoted

to the ethos represented by Robert Browning were visually replicated in this center for the study of "officially correct" art.
Furthermore, the Parisian environment bolstered Frank's already
strong interest in medieval French life; Jean Froissart's *Chronicles*
(1400), with its compelling images of fourteenth-century knightly
derring-do, were a long-term inspiration to him. He spent many an
hour sketching the collection of armor at the Musée de l'Armée, and
the "salon machine" he attempted while in Paris was an enormous
canvas depicting the Battle of Crécy described by Froissart.

B.F. tired early of the art-focused sojourn-in-progress and returned alone to America. Gertrude and Charles remained for awhile
but later left Frank on his own. "Student Life in Paris" (1900) reveals
that he enjoyed the bohemian life; with the bank drafts arriving regularly and with freedom from parental pressures, he had a fine time
of it.[6] Eventually, however, he abandoned his masterwork. The
canvas was rolled up, lowered to the street with a rope, and carried
off by fellow San Franciscan Ernest Peixotto. His father soon called
him home, impatient with Frank's trifling.

From Painting to Storytelling

The trifling, though, was of a particularly significant kind. The cause
for B.F.'s impatience was the series of stories, rather than the
sketches and paintings he was paying to have produced, that Frank
was sending to the younger brother who missed him. Their bond
had been particularly strong, as is suggested in the dedication of *The
Pit* to Charles: "IN MEMORY OF CERTAIN LAMENTABLE TALES OF THE ROUND
(DINING-ROOM) TABLE HEROES; OF THE EPIC OF THE PEWTER PLATOONS, AND
THE ROMANCE CYCLE OF 'GASTON LE FOX,' WHICH WE INVENTED, MAINTAINED
AND FOUND MARVELLOUS AT THE TIME WHEN WE BOTH WERE BOYS."[7] To use
Norris's own term, Frank and Charles were *born* story-
tellers – although Gertrude's incessant literariness suggests that
nurture may have been at least as influential as nature.[8] Norris would
fail as a painter only to realize his true talent before his readership of
one. "Thus it was that his first novel, 'Robert d'Artois,' was written,"
explained Charles in 1914; "he loved story-telling, and his imagination knew no limits."[9] As the installments concerning Gaston *de Foix*
(prominent in Froissart and celebrated in a set of relief sculptures at

the South Kensington Museum) arrived, Norris was producing his first of several serializations.

This now-lost manuscript was never published, but an article derived from his study of medieval armor, "Clothes of Steel," appeared, self-illustrated, in the *San Francisco Chronicle* of 31 March 1889.[10] At 19, and at a time when a bachelor's degree was not a requisite for a writing career, Norris found himself at home, an academically unqualified applicant for admission to the University of California at Berkeley. He was unwittingly moving toward a four-year period of dabbling in higher education; rather than beginning in earnest the apprenticeship that he would inevitably have to serve in 1896-98, he enjoyed an extension of the leisurely sojourn in the world of art that had been his Paris experience.

Yvernelle: The Indiscretions of Youth

Gertrude's son had returned from Paris a stylish dandy – something of a velvet-jacketed lounge lizard like the artists Presley in *The Octopus* and Corthell in *The Pit*. Through the years at Berkeley, he remained artistic and, at moments, resembled a young aesthete as poems such as "Brunehilde" and "Les Enerves de Jumieges" appeared over the nom de plume "Norrys."[11] Norris illustrated college publications with his drawings, executed cover designs, wrote parodies of the writers studied in his composition course, contributed stories and a play to the *Blue and Gold* yearbook, and acted in skits and plays. During his sophomore year in 1891, his first book appeared – a lavishly illustrated, richly bound volume issued in time for Christmas gift-book sales.

Yvernelle: A Legend of Feudal France[12] is a metrical verse romance redolent with the spirit of Sir Walter Scott and singled out for special honor by the local bluestockings, who displayed it in 1893 at the San Francisco Women's Literary Exhibit at the World Columbian Exhibition in Chicago. Gertrude must have been beside herself with pride. The father of the poet, on the other hand, made frequent references to Norris's "thimble-headed bobism" as a writer, according to Charles. Philistine though he was, B. F. Norris's intolerance of his son's early efforts has since been approximated by many more sophisticated readers of *Yvernelle*, who have understandably had

trouble in developing an appreciation of such an old-style piece of
writing from an author normally envisioned as "modern." It is easier
to imagine one of Gertrude's generation as the author of *Yvernelle*.
Indeed, Norris "buried" the work, so that reviewers of his later novels were unaware of it.

In conventionally archaic poetic diction and bouncing octosyl-
labic lines, Norris describes the virginal maiden Yvernelle long
smitten with love for the gallant Sir Caverlaye, who is drawn back to
her after a long absence abroad. The predictable development sets
the melodrama in forward motion: as in all Romantic Love literature,
the lovers face an impediment to their union. Sir Caverlaye is not so
inexperienced in matters amorous as the naive Yvernelle. His sojourn to a distant land included an intimate relationship with the
passionate Guhaldrada, from whom he has parted in a less than
courteous manner – rejecting the woman who has given her heart,
and more, to him. Guhaldrada's passion – like that of her prototype,
Racine's Phèdre – floods into a less attractive channel. Enraged by
rejection, the dark beauty pronounces a curse: the maiden he next
kisses will suffer ruin.

Sir Caverlaye, now ready to give himself to one he loves as a
knight should, suddenly recalls the curse: true love requires that he
save Yvernelle by avoiding her; he must now pine for the unobtain-
able maiden; Yvernelle is beside herself with grief, and she decides
to enter a convent. All is not lost, however, for Sir Caverlaye finally
sees the means to the end he prefers. To discharge the curse, he
need only kiss *another* woman – for example, Guhaldrada herself.
This he does, but almost too late. Yvernelle is scheduled to pro-
nounce her vows as a bride to Christ. Sir Caverlaye pushes his noble
steed to the limit, dashing across the countryside and arriving at the
very last moment. Love flowers at last, and one assumes that – unlike
Norris's parents – the hero and heroine live happily ever after.

Briefly – and to his credit – it *was* a beginning for Norris. He
had failed to win gridiron glory and to produce a painting that might
take salon honors in Paris. But he had succeeded at writing, and, it
should be added, the several reviews that appeared were favorable.
Viewed objectively as the chivalric romance literature it is, *Yvernelle*
is not an inferior example.

Finding a More Masculine and Contemporary Voice

At the same time that Norris – at age 21 – was realizing his mother's ideal conception of a son as college man and artist, a personality adjustment *was* occurring in him. Another side of his nature was emerging, for at Berkeley few fraternity men were as ferociously involved in the society as he became. The gloves and cane were put in the closet and some "regular guy" socialization began: the frat house became increasingly more central. Indeed, Norris's present fame outside of literary and historical circles includes his creation of a special annual dinner staged by the brothers of Phi Gamma Delta, still called "the Norris." Kissing the roasted whole pig as it was carried ritualistically into the banquet hall was part of the rubric he devised. Had not B.F. already alienated himself from the family, he might have approved wholeheartedly of such a sounding of the manly note after so long a delay. He might also have approved of Frank, while still a student, placing short stories in *real* magazines, such as *Overland Monthly* and *Argonaut*. As far as we know, Norris had still not known the rigors of holding a part-time job. But these were the first businesslike signs of professional success. Finally, however, B.F. had more cause for lowering his brows at the close of the Berkeley years: in 1894, his son failed to receive a degree with his classmates.

Three years earlier, in 1891, Norris had petitioned the university to waive the standard course requirements that were his undoing. He declared that he had already determined as his the career of professional writer, including an early review of *Yvernelle* to prove the seriousness of his claim.[13] It did not work, and in the summer of 1894 he appears to have thought that Harvard University, with its innovative "elective" orientation toward higher education, might be more suitable for him. He was wrong about that. He never received a degree. But in the fall, accompanied by Gertrude and Charles, he settled in Cambridge, Massachusetts, soon taking a dormitory room on campus. That year he again did what he liked, completing three courses in French literature. He also enrolled in a two-semester course conducted by Lewis E. Gates, during which he received instruction on the craft of writing and produced 45 surviving "themes," indicating that he was at work on material related to three later published novels: *McTeague, Blix,* and *Vandover*. The themes dramatized the change that had been wrought during the Berkeley years. His fixation on things medieval had gradually dissipated itself after the publication of *Yvernelle* and a bit of gothic supernaturalism that appeared in *The Wave* in 1891, "The Jongleur of Taillebois." "The Son of the Sheik" (1891) and "Lauth" (1893) are two other improbable short stories of the same order – although they did represent an intellectual advance.[14] Both reflect an awareness of concepts generally related to contemporaneous discussions of evolutionary theory and possibly the influence of the evolutionary metaphysician and moralist, Professor Joseph LeConte, on the Berkeley campus. But in a series of five *Overland Monthly* stories sharing the main title "Outward and Visible Signs," one can see most clearly Norris's act of separating himself from the tastes of his mother's generation and what *Yvernelle* had signified.[15] The tone of these short stories published in 1894-95 was smart and up to date, and the focus was on 1890s social life among upper-class young men and women. The influence of sophisticated stylists such as Anthony Hope and Richard Harding Davis was quite apparent as Norris began to produce snappy dialogue for readers of the kind to which F. Scott Fitzgerald would later appeal in his popular magazine fiction. While writing such light pieces anticipating the often-bantering *Blix*, Norris's simultaneous development in another direction also shows in the Harvard themes, where one sees the influence of Emile Zola and Guy de Maupassant. His new tendency was especially clear in the theme for 22 April 1895:

> It was in an alley behind a big hotel, and the man, an old man, with a battered derby hat that had turned green, was drunk; blind drunk, reeling about as if in the forecastle of a wreck, running his head stupidly against the side of the houses, trying to hold on by the wheels of old carts and by the sides of manure bins. He was looking for the flask he had dropped and a group of hack men and cab-drivers at the mouth of the alley were watching him, laughing and very amused because he couldn't find it. Bye and bye the man came down, full length, helpless as a falling tree and lay prone and inert, face downwards, blowing his fetid breath into the mud and the filth of the alley.[16]

There was no manure in *Yvernelle* or the "Outward and Visible Signs" stories, nor did its characters wallow like brutes in the filth. Norris was now making selections from the French menu as well as the Anglo-American.

A New Ploy: The Travel Writer as Manly Adventurer

When Norris returned to San Francisco that summer, he was preparing a collection of his short stories for Coryell & Co. of New York[17] and continuing to write the Zolaesque *McTeague* and *Vandover*. He also devised a plan to accelerate his progress as a professional author, following the example of the immensely successful travel writer, Richard Harding Davis. He would visit South Africa, trek northward to Egypt, and sail back to America via the Strait of Gibraltar – writing local color articles along the way. He departed from San Francisco on 28 October 1895, and, before he dispatched one word to the newspaper with which he had an arrangement, the *San Francisco Chronicle*, he was in the limelight. Or, rather, he was sharing it with the ubiquitous Gertrude who granted interviews with journalists regarding her son's mysterious disappearance between England and South Africa. The devoted, distraught mother; the favorite son with an unpredictable artistic temperament: it was a journalist's dream.[18]

The delay in cabling his mother from South Africa was related to an extraordinary coincidence. Norris was traveling with a group planning to participate in an English attempt to topple the Boer government, Cecil Rhodes's strategy for British appropriation of South African gold and diamond mines. As Norris sent the first of his essays on local conditions, the Jameson Raid occurred. Norris became involved with one of the conspirators, San Franciscan mining engineer John Hays Hammond; served as a messenger in a British uniform; and was incarcerated and deported on the coup's failure. Perhaps, then, there was more of B.F. in him than he suspected: he was certainly behaving like the "real man" seen in the most virile adventure tales; he had faced death in a uniform and also on the sickbed when brought down by "African fever." He even returned to San Francisco with a snake tattoo.

The Wave: The Protracted Apprenticeship

When he disembarked in New York City after his African jaunt, Norris was moving forward as a writer, it was clear, but he was soon to experience two major failures. The agreement with Coryell & Co. to publish a collection of stories fell through. What was also soon evident was that the South African sketches would not pay off as hoped. The eight that appeared in the *Chronicle* were not reprinted nationally. A ninth had been published in the national-circulation *Harper's Weekly* but received no more attention than a tenth published locally in *The Wave*.[19] The next step was down, rather than up. In April 1896, Norris became a salaried staff writer and, as editor John O'Hara Cosgrave phrased it to Franklin Walker, "editorial assistant" for the same regional weekly, *The Wave*. From writing fiction to reporting to preparing advertisements, Norris appears to have served a full apprenticeship. Two years and more than 165 *Wave* pieces later, Norris finally escaped from the drudgery of working for Cosgrave.[20]

As Franklin Walker noted, 1897 was marked by depression for Norris (Walker, 144). It was also characterized by rage born of feelings of impotence owing to his lack of success at age 27: the failures were mounting. In a memoir written three decades later, Norris's friend Bruce Porter (the stained-glass artist and Swedenborgian aesthete who served as the model for Vanamee in *The Octopus* and Sheldon Corthell in *The Pit*) recalled an angry outburst when Norris learned of the success in the East enjoyed by old friend and fellow *Wave* writer Gelett Burgess.[21] The Wildean author of a bit of doggerel entitled "The Purple Cow" had tickled the nation and won acclaim. His *Vivette* would be published later that year, while Norris remained churning out copy for a West Coast weekly of limited circulation. Indeed, Norris is likely to have suffered something akin to a nervous breakdown during the early spring of 1897 – given his absence from work from mid-March to mid-May and some peculiar self-revelations made in his *Wave* writings on his return.

"Little Dramas of the Curbstone," for example, includes three sketches, one of which, it might be opined, Cosgrave should not have given the editorial nod. In it Norris describes his hysterical response to a young boy born blind and deaf. He candidly confesses an urge to attack the "imbecile" with his cane and beat the life out of him. Why he should feel this urge, he does not explain. In another article, "The Sailing of the *Excelsior*," he tells of seeing an alcoholic asleep on a wharf and describes his rage to discover a man so despicable. His desire, expressed without tongue in cheek, is to throw the man off the wharf and let him perish. Less murderous but as violent is the tone of "An Opening for Novelists" from the same period.[22]

Burgess and his whimsical fellow artists known as Les Jeunes are cause for outrage; so also is their too-precious magazine, *The Lark*, which embodied the aestheticism of *The Yellow Book* and *The Chap Book* as it parodied it. *The Lark* is the token of what Norris finds contemptible: the childishness of artistic self-indulgence, the avoidance of serious reflection on human nature for the sake of cultivating the pretty, and the preference for the artificial over the dynamism of real life. Norris was rejecting not only the triumph of the trivial in such works as "The Purple Cow" but the androgynous dilettantism of such "friends" in the fine arts as Burgess, Bruce Porter, and Ernest Peixotto. Guilt by association as much as the frustration of being stalled in his career thus lies behind this cruel outburst, for Norris was as devoted to "the fine arts" as they. Indeed, bookbinding would later replace the design of covers for college publications as an avocation of his, and it was his taste that resulted in the bindings of *The Octopus* and *The Pit* being modeled on that of Henry James's *What Maisie Knew* (1897) (*Letters*, 135).

The manly note is here self-consciously sounded as he calls for a more red-blooded, vigorous response to the artistic possibilities of life in San Francisco: "Give us stories now, give us men, strong, brutal men, with red-hot blood in 'em, with unleashed passions rampant in 'em, blood and bones and viscera in 'em." In this psychologically complex piece, Norris was rejecting the "feminine" or "artsy" cultural values Les Jeunes represented, as well as the delicate aesthetic values that were Gertrude's. (He was still living with his mother at age 27.) Identifying with more forceful, masculine role-models such as Zola, Robert Louis Stevenson, and Rudyard Kipling ("A qui le tour, who shall be our Kipling?"), he was as impatient with the "thimble-headed bobism" of artistes as his father had been. At the same time, though, Norris was Norris: the Gallic show of Burgess-like sophistication, *A qui le tour?*, is a revealing anomaly amidst the testosterone-suffused rhetoric and the vulgarity of "blood and bones and viscera in 'em."

The psychological factors noted may not, however, have been the only causes of the crisis. B.F. suffered from what Kathleen Thompson Norris once described as "his nervous troubles."[23] She did not go into detail, but the son's problem in 1897 may have been more than psychological. In "Metropolitan Noises," published shortly after Norris's return to *The Wave* in May, he writes in detail about the "positive physical torture" of San Francisco's street noises for individuals suffering from a "nervous complaint."[24] The choice of subject and the specifics provided suggest that he had firsthand experience of symptoms then diagnosed as those of neurasthenia. Thus, the two-month absence from *The Wave* that spring receives a likely explanation: the prescribed treatment at the time was the "rest cure" popularized by Dr. S. Weir Mitchell and criticized by Charlotte Perkins Gilman via the now well-known short story, "The Yellow Wallpaper" (1892).

Unlike the heroine of that tale of progressive insanity, however, Norris recovered. He made amends for his attack on Les Jeunes, reestablishing his friendships with Porter and Peixotto. That they were reconciled with Norris suggests that they knew of mitigating circumstances. That the thin-skinned Burgess – who pasted Norris's attack in his scrapbook – let bygones be bygones doubly suggests the same.[25] Norris had simply not been himself for a season. Furthermore, while Norris called for a more dynamic literature commensurate with rough-and-tumble environment that was the San Francisco being pictured in his *McTeague* manuscript, he returned to his old ways: the series of Justin Sturgis-Leander dialogues he soon commenced for *The Wave* were droll bits of harmless high-society patter – a specialty of the lately lambasted Gelett Burgess.[26] The crisis had passed, and by December Norris made clear in *The Wave* his new resolve to succeed, picturing in *"Happiness by Conquest"*[27] his hero as the individual who persists in the face of adversity to *make* his own success – by sheer willpower.

Renewed Ambition: The California Kipling

Norris had good reason for restored confidence by the end of 1897. That spring and summer he had published some of the best short fictions of his career. "Judy's Service of Gold Plate" and "Fantaisie Printaniere" – both spin-offs from the *McTeague* manuscript – were brilliant comic descents into the "low-life" neighborhoods of San Francisco.[28] "The Strangest Thing" and "The House with the Blinds" offered engagingly executed mysteries, but much better was "The Third Circle," which takes the high-toned *Wave* readership into the nethermost recesses of Chinatown, where opium-addicted Caucasian prostitutes flourish and the debutante-heroine, who had mysteriously disappeared at the beginning of the story, is discovered years later as a hag in "white slavery."[29] More conventional were the comic tall tales " 'Boom' " and "Shorty Stack, Pugilist" – in which Norris showed his proficiency in producing salable, chuckle-inducing entertainments.[30] His penchant for the bizarre resurfaced, however, in "The Associated Un-Charities," in which – as in *McTeague* – he tested what of his experimental imagination readers would tolerate. This is a comic tale, featuring Justin Sturgis and Leander, in which the latter young gentleman shows the "Mr. Hyde" side of his otherwise eminently Victorian personality.[31] The victims of the little joke he arranges happen to be three men who are vulnerable because of a physical handicap: they are blind. The comic tale becomes a chilling account of victimization, and one suddenly realizes that Norris has transformed it into a mordant indictment of the insensitive social group to which Leander belongs. Perhaps, too, he recalled his own reaction to the "imbecile" in "Little Dramas."

The same kind of artful reversal occurs in "His Dead Mother's Portrait," in which a night on the town for some carefree young gents ends in the discovery that the presumed-dead mother of one of them is a dancer in the disreputable "dive" Bella Union. Norris could entertain as when he whimsically imagined an Olympics for cyclists in "A Bicycle Gymkhana," but there was a need to move beyond the glittering surfaces of the Gay Nineties to depict the less than attractive complexities that are at the core of his serious writings – for instance, in the grimly Schopenhauerian fable of "The Puppets and the Puppy," also published in 1897.[32]

Norris's Probatory Orientation

Getting beneath the surface of things is an apparent motivation throughout the Norris canon and a primary explanation for the psychological and sociological exposé writing counterpointing with his more conventional love tales, comic yarns, and local color articles. It also elucidates Norris's conception of himself as a "Romantic" writer, which has complicated the task of more than one literary historian sensitive to signs of loyalty in his fiction to the opposed school of Realism. Norris eventually clarified his complex view of the relationship between Romanticism, Realism, and Naturalism. In some of his book reviews and literary essays of the *Wave* years, however, he heightens the apparent paradox of a realistically oriented writer identifying with Romantics. In 1896, for example, he celebrated William Dean Howells's treatment of the "ultimate physical relation of man and woman" in *A Parting and a Meeting*; Howells displayed "the greatest subtlety and finesse," Norris asserts as he reveals an unqualified appreciation of the Realistic literary method Howells used. The next year he identified Howells's *A Modern Instance* as the "greatest" representation of modern American life in fiction. And yet Howellsian Realism did not suffice. As Norris also explained in "Zola as a Romantic Writer," Howells the Realist did not delve far enough *into* life; he limited himself to "average" experience and thus stayed too much on the surface of everyday life.[33] Norris, inspired by the unreserved Zola, had no intention of discreetly stopping where Howells did.

Zola, in contrast to Howells, did not limit his extravagantly fertile imagination in his compelling quests for the profoundest truths of life. Furthermore, he took brave risks with reader credibility as he dared to move beyond the commonplace and to treat the exotic and bizarre – the subjects of Romantic writers. Zola not only mapped accurately the conditions in the modern socioeconomic order but plumbed the depths of the monstrously grotesque, the irrational, and even the disgusting in human experience – without regard to the Victorian proprieties that Howells observed and that Norris himself was then violating in the manuscripts of *McTeague* and *Vandover*. Imaginatively inducing broader truths from all manner of data, Zola went beyond the limits that Anglo-American Realists had, in his view, needlessly imposed on themselves. And thus the theme of Norris's "Zola's *Rome*"[34] and "Zola as a Romantic Writer" in 1896: Zola's often cited Naturalism does not represent an "inner circle" of Realism, as many critics think; it is a vibrant revival of the probatory Romantic tradition that attempted to articulate the *whole* of what Nature might reveal about itself. Norris would redefine Naturalism in 1901 as a synthesis of Realism and Romanticism rather than an extension of the latter, but his essential concept and orientation remained the same. Zolaesque Naturalism was the intellectual and aesthetic justification for a daring exercise of both imagination and reason in Norris's many debunkings of the false and revelations of the true.

Acknowledging the Unattractive in Human Nature

Norris's probatory approach to human experience during the *Wave* years is nowhere more apparent than in "Reversion to Type" (1897) and "A Case for Lombroso" (1897), which at first may appear merely outlandish fictions.[35] Both feature characters whose personalities are radically altered when both degenerate from a socially well-adjusted condition to a madly criminal state – of the kind that the well-known criminologist Cesare Lombroso then interpreted as genetically determined. One may be tempted to dismiss them as mere reworkings of the fanciful "atavistic lapse" theme Norris first treated as a freshman at Berkeley in the improbable "Son of the Sheik" – a story in which a college-educated sophisticate under stress lapses to his hereditarily preserved identity as an Arab warrior. These later stories, however, are not related to a popular *theory* about evolutionary regression but a more sensational *fact* reported by Norris in *The Wave* of 6 March 1897. What had caught his eye were newspaper reports of one John M. Oakley – a respectable millionaire who had heretofore led a most exemplary life – drinking himself to death in the company of a prostitute at the Palace Hotel in San Francisco: "A strange, hideous end of an upright life; a case, perhaps, for our friend Lombroso."[36]

It was Norris, however, who took the Oakley case, analyzed it, and spun out tales prompting the conclusion that respectability and other appearances of civilization may prove either veneerlike or revelatory of only particular dimensions of multifaceted human nature. In the real-life incident and the two tales, we see an anarchic second personality within the self conditioned to socially proper behavior – an amoral, barbaric, and perhaps bestial dimension of human nature that has not been eliminated despite centuries of civilizing influence. Norris was focusing on what his contemporary Sigmund Freud would term the *id*. While few might have the unpredictably extravagant experience of debauchery that Oakley did, what was predictable was that equally refined individuals might feel *some* pressure from that primitive second self within, no matter how often or vigorously proper Victorians denied these impulses.

Because Zola had already explored this fictional territory in work after work, one finds an undeniable instance of intertextuality here. And yet Norris himself had passed through an Oakley-like crisis that spring when, facing the specter of failure in his chosen career, he had run amok, bristling with violence directed at his friends and generally behaving like an unsociable brute. Whatever the exact ratio between external influence and internal impetus, Norris had established the question that he would pose again and again: Why do people behave the way they do, often to their detriment?

The Call from New York City

In the fall of 1897, Norris finally completed *McTeague*, a portrait he began sketching after reading in the newspapers of 1893 one of those un-Howellsian occurrences of the abnormal: the stabbing to death of a Mrs. Collins by her drunken brute of a husband. Norris was also working on a study of the abnormal experience of a young man named Vandover who – although born to the manor like Norris – was degenerating into a literal brute largely owing to, ironically, the influences of the Victorian moral environment in which he had been reared. Both novels demonstrated that Norris was correct in "Zola as a Romantic Writer": in the extraordinary, behind-the-scenes occurrences of life *were* to be found the means of generating great literature. But while Norris's short fiction writing had markedly improved, 1898 began without his obtaining a publisher for a second planned volume of stories, *Ways That Are Dark*.[37] *Vandover* was not yet complete, and *McTeague* did not find a publisher. At this point, the son of B. F. Norris made a shrewd business decision. *McTeague* might be a wonderful piece of progressive artistry, but he needed a guaranteed trump card, a mass-appeal eye-catcher like Richard Harding Davis's *Soldiers of Fortune* (1897) to escape from *The Wave*. He would write a formula book with special variations that would distinguish itself from the run-of-the-mill adventure. Thus, on 8 January 1898, *Moran of the Lady Letty* began its serialization in *The Wave*.

As the weekly installments appeared, Norris mailed them off to companies like the S. S. McClure syndicate. It worked. By the middle of February he was on his way to the publishing Mecca, hired to work in New York for that syndicate and *McClure's Magazine*. Here the story of Norris's life changes: this was the beginning of real success, because he would also be connected with the book publishing firm of Doubleday & McClure Co. And there was one other important development: situated on West 33rd Street in New York City, he was no longer living with his mother. For the first time, he was a self-supporting individual and a continent away from the woman who needed so much psychological support from him.

Chapter Two

Moran of the Lady Letty

In May 1897, Norris declared in "An Opening for Novelists" that the opportunities for striking short stories appeared limitless for an observant San Franciscan choosing to "go a-gunning for stories up and down our streets and into our houses and parlors and lodging houses and saloons and dives and along our wharves and into our theaters." Like other *Wave* writers who repeatedly articulated this point, Norris concluded that – in San Francisco at least – truth *is* often "stranger than fiction": the writer needs only pay close attention to find life offering almost ready-made tales of the most sensational kind.

He had not changed his mind on this when, for the first issue of the 1898 *Wave*, he turned to the composition of the installments of *Moran* against weekly press deadlines. As in the 1897 short stories "The Third Circle" and "His Dead Mother's Portrait," Norris immediately exploited the city's sensational character and particularly the lurid history of the waterfront area. Indeed, when lecturing the city's aesthetes in "An Opening for Novelists," he had identified in his first example what would become the locally available *donnée* for *Moran*:

> While you are rounding a phrase a sailor has been shanghaied down there along the water front; while you are sustaining a metaphor, another See Yup has been hatcheted yonder in Gambler's Alley; a man has time to be stabbed while you are composing a villanelle; the crisis of a life has come and gone while you have been niggling with your couplet. "Murder and sudden death" [i.e., too melodramatic], say you? Yes, but it's the life that lives; it's reality, it's the thing that counts.[1]

Shanghaiing did occur in the waterfront dives. "A Story of Adventure off the California Coast" (*Moran*'s subtitle) could credibly begin thus.[2] Furthermore, that the hero could be reported in the newspapers as having disappeared "from the face of the earth," while he

was experiencing manly adventure in an exotic locale, squared with
Norris's own experience during his jaunt to South Africa in 1895-96.

From Theory to Practice: Tonal Inconsistencies

Eight months after "An Opening" appeared, however, Norris had
mixed feelings as he began to move toward the point at which the
drugged hero would be dropped through a trap door in the floor of
one of those dives and then carried out to a veritable pirate ship. He
had to proceed in order to produce a "rattling good yarn" of the
kind that would attract the attention of an eastern publisher and
make possible his entry into the world of professional novel writing – and he did. But along the way his handling of the task varied.
Straightforward romancing sometimes modulated into parody of the
genre. His attitude toward the imagined middle-brow readership he
had to please veered toward contempt as he satirized its tastes. Serious reflections on precivilized human nature unexpectedly appeared
in the midst of flamboyantly melodramatic action sequences. That he
was not sure where he was going to take his hero and heroine as he
wrote the immediately published episodes also shows in *Moran*'s
irregular design.

Norris's uneasiness about stooping to obtain approval from the
"average reader" was again clear after *Moran* was published in book
form in September 1898: he sheepishly accepted praise from William
Dean Howells while explaining that such literary kite flying would be
transcended by the soon-to-be published *McTeague* (*Letters*, 60). In
late December 1897, though, Norris was already uncomfortable
about the immediate response to *Moran* by professional peers and
close friends in San Francisco. He had quite condescendingly articulated the sophisticated values that might be turned against him
when explaining the failure of a play in June 1897. He found *The
Question* a subtle, witty satire that might have succeeded with a less
numbskulled audience: "such a play . . . presupposes . . . an intelligence that can find more pleasure in an exchange of wit than in an
exchange of blows, that rejoices in the thrust of a keenly-pointed
satire rather than in that of the assassin's knife."[3] In short, Norris
knew the difference between fine taste and the cruder appetite of
the public that bought the many prose tales featuring the thrust of

the assassin's knife – and that, he hoped, would be satisfied by *Moran*. It was not coincidental, then, that *Moran* was his only longer work that began in so self-conscious a manner. Aware as he started that he would be seen by his peers as indulging in rank melodrama, he paraphrased the litany in the Episcopalian Book of Common Prayer – "from battle and murder, and from sudden death, *Good Lord, deliver us*" – to inform fellow sophisticates that he knew what he was about. "This is to be," he began with a wink to those in the know, "a story of a battle, at least one murder, and several sudden deaths" (*M*, 1).

His second sentence was just as self-conscious. It acknowledged that a fanciful artifice was deliberately being constructed and that he was following a formula suitable for his adventure-loving readership. That a tale of battle, murder, and sudden death began at Miss Josie Herrick's home "with a pink tea and among the mingled odors of many delicate perfumes and the hale, frank smell of Caroline Testout roses" (*M*, 1) was wholly appropriate. The readers he envisioned for his melodrama were the denizens of polite society like Josie who, in such drawing rooms, vicariously participated in fictionally distanced mayhem and star-driven lovemaking. A major appeal of popular romance is that it offers the proper a penalty-free immersion in impropriety.

An End to Effeteness and the Beginnings of Maturation

Ross Wilbur is introduced at Josie's reception. He is an effeminate young gentleman engaging in polite conversation while refreshing himself with chocolate and stuffed olives: "They sat down and talked in a window recess for a moment, Wilbur toeing-in absurd fashion as he tried to make a lap for his plate" (*M*, 3). Departing, this simpering avatar of San Francisco's leisure class faces what is, for him, a crisis measuring his diminutive life: "I wonder what I'm going to do with myself until supper-time" (*M*, 6). Finding a note from Jerry Haight at his club, he decides that it would be amusing to loaf about the waterfront while waiting for Jerry's ship to arrive. When a Barbary Coast tough invites him to share a drink, Ross reflects that such a lark would be even more amusing. The drugged drink quaffed, Ross is

carried to the *Bertha Millner*. Once aboard and impressed as a
common seaman, Ross – like the boyish hero of Kipling's *Captains
Courageous* (1897) – is immediately introduced to the rough-and-
tumble world of virility.

The rabidly aggressive Captain Kitchell is his first mentor. Ridi-
culing Ross as a "lily of the valley" pantywaist, this uncivilized
creature who is dominant in this extrasocial, Darwinian context rein-
forces his lessons in a direct manner when Ross protests:

> "Look here," he began, "I – "
> The captain knocked him down with a blow of one enormous fist
> upon the mouth, and while he was yet stretched upon the deck kicked him
> savagely in the stomach. Then he allowed him to rise, caught him by the neck
> and the slack of his overcoat, and ran him forward to where a hatchway, not
> two feet across, opened in the deck. Without ado he flung him down into the
> darkness below. (*M*, 17-18)

Before the close of chapter 1, that is, Norris was already exceeding
anything of the kind to be found in such works as Anthony Hope's
wildly successful *Prisoner of Zenda* (1894). And he would continue
in this manner, giving the readers of Josie's class precisely what magazine and book sales indicated they wanted, and then some.

Lying in the hold of the *Bertha Millner*, Ross has no choice but
to cooperate with Captain Kitchell and conform to the rule of might
makes right. Thus, while he "went down the forward hatch at the toe
of Kitchell's boot – silk-hatted, melton-overcoated, patent-booted,
and gloved in suedes," he reappears a changed man: "Two minutes
later there emerged upon the deck a figure in oilskins and a
sou'wester. There was blood upon the face of him and the grime of
an unclean ship upon his bare hands. It was Wilbur, and yet not
Wilbur" (*M*, 19). Despite his high-toned background, the new life
among the Chinese crew proves bracing for Ross – and a welcome
escape from the endless round of cotillions and yachting parties.
Wholly novel experiences abound, as do unpredictable responses by
Ross. He feels, for example, a rush of adrenaline when the piratical
Kitchell spies a derelict bark to be salvaged. The embodiment of ra-
pacious greed, Kitchell becomes manic, "positively trembling from
head to foot." His enthusiasm is contagious: it "was impossible to
resist the excitement of the situation" (*M*, 61). Ross thus takes his
first large step away from citified androgyny toward "manhood": he

rises, or descends, to the captain's level, joining forces with a man who proudly proclaims, "I'm hog right through . . . ninety-nine swine an' me make a hundred swine. . . . If that bark's abandoned, an' I says she is, she's ours" (*M*, 60-61). Ross proves that he is not yet "a shoat, with both feet in the trough," though, when it turns out that the *Lady Letty* has not been abandoned.

Gender Confusion at Sea

Enter Moran of the *Lady Letty*, who at first appears a sailor in a slicker, unconscious from the gas produced by an explosion. Ross tends to this sole survivor after Kitchell has left and, upon observing a deep inhalation, makes another discovery. Norris again goes beyond the limits in popular romance as chapter 3 concludes with Ross observing the sailor's swelling neck and breast: "My God, it's a girl!" (*M*, 69). And what a "girl" she proves. She is as androgynous as the orchid-like hero of chapter 1.

Moran Sternersen is *not* the typical helpless heroine of an 1890s romance or even related to the liberated "New Woman" figure typed by Hope Langham in Richard Harding Davis's *Soldiers of Fortune*. Rather, so bizarre is her conception that she appears as Norris's revenge on the "Young Girl" readership to whose genteel cheek one was not supposed to bring a blush. With Moran, Norris not only provides sensation sufficient for any romance reader but vandalizes virtually all genteel concepts of noble womanhood imaginable. Via Moran, for example, he raises the unsettling question of whether the brutelike traits of a Captain Kitchell might possibly reside within the breast of the fairer sex – a question Zola had long since answered in the affirmative, to the outrage of Ruskinesque idealists.

While Moran is recovering from the effects of the gas, Kitchell, "a very wolf within the scent of its prey," begins to loot the *Lady Letty*. The new Ross Wilbur is "not far behind him in eagerness," and Norris accounts for the emergence of a similarly brutelike personality within him: "Somewhere deep down in the heart of every Anglo-Saxon lies the predatory instinct of his Viking ancestors – an instinct that a thousand years of respectability and tax-paying have not quite succeeded in eliminating" (*M*, 74). Yet, as Ross discovers that Moran is the heir to the ship, his civilized self becomes dominant again: he

is worried that, when Kitchell learns that the *Lady Letty* belongs to
her, he will murder her and do worse, given "the question of
Moran's sex" (*M*, 83). Kitchell soon drowns during a sudden squall
and so the unmentionable in popular romances – rape – is not attempted, but it is debatable whether Moran *could* have been
violated by him.

This doughty maiden of Irish and Norwegian extraction quickly
proves to have more of the stuff of *her* Viking ancestors in her than
Ross. When the squall threatens the *Bertha Millner* and immobilizes
the terrified male crew, her voice blares raucously through the wind
"like the call of a bugle." She does not sound at all like a romantic
heroine: "And you call yourselves sailor men! Are you going to
drown like rats on a plank?" (*M*, 91). Barking orders and intimidating
the sailors into action, *she* saves the schooner. Second, she does not
look or act like Princess Flavia of *The Prisoner of Zenda* the next
morning: "She was still wearing men's clothing . . . and was booted
to the knee; but now she wore no hat, and her enormous mane of
rye-colored hair was braided into long strands near to the thickness
of a man's arm. The redness of her face gave a startling effect to her
pale blue eyes and sandy, heavy eyebrows, that easily lowered to a
frown. She ate with her knife, and after pushing away her plate
Wilbur observed that she drank half a tumbler of whiskey and water"
(*M*, 96). Sizing up Ross, she smites the table with her red fist in
hearty laughter as she learns that Kitchell had actually shanghaied
such a runt.

Norris repeatedly comes back to and dwells upon the incon-
gruities of his heroine who "drank whiskey after her meals, and
when angry, which was often, swore like a buccaneer" (*M*, 104).
"This schooner smells like a dead Jew" is one of her choice expres-
sions in the *Wave* version later bowdlerized.[4] We also note that this
woman given to hauling around barrels on the deck has a tattoo on
her arm. It will not be easy to win her love, although that must occur
somehow, because a popular romance *must* include "love interest."
Ross, therefore, soon comes to the conclusion that she is "a ripping
fine girl." Realizing that he is smitten, he rhapsodizes in the manner
of   Norris's   heroes   in   more   conventional   love   stories:
"you're – you're splendid. There in the squall last evening, when you
stood at the wheel, with your hair – " But Moran is not Josie: " 'Oh,

drop that!' said the girl, contemptuously, and went up on deck. Wilbur followed, scratching an ear" (*M*, 101).

The Gender-Free "Brute-Within"

Their unchaperoned adventures together begin. They sail to Magdalena Bay in Baja California to fish for shark whose livers will be turned into "cod-liver oil" for sale in San Francisco. Ross is undaunted by Moran's rejection of his affection; in fact, he soon moves beyond Platonic sentiment to randiness when he passes her and is "made aware that her hair, her neck, her entire personality exhaled a fine, sweet, natural redolence" (*M*, 104-5). In the bay at night, they share the mysterious experience of their schooner rising out of the water; they later learn that gray whales have merely been rubbing their backs on the keel, but the apparently supernatural occurrence is enough to make their superstitious crew abandon ship. Chinese cutthroats – Kai-gingh, who are "the wickedest breed of cats that ever cut teeth" (*M*, 141) – then enter the bay in a junk. Ross and Moran work with them to cut up a dead sperm whale from which both parties can turn a quick profit. Moran discovers that it contains a treasure in ambergris; the pirates scent it as they are departing; the *Bertha Millner* springs a leak, and Moran and Ross are overtaken, losing the ambergris to the barbarous Hoang and his equally violent crew. Their adventure continuing on shore after Moran washes the blood from her hair and they begin to repair their schooner, Ross is "admiring" Moran more and more. He has to check himself one night when they are sleeping on the beach, as Norris once again violates the limits of propriety. As Moran slept, Ross "leaned toward her, so close that he could catch the savor of her breath and the smell of her neck, warm with sleep . . . and it seemed to him as if her bare arm, flung out at full length, had some sweet aroma of its own" (*M*, 175). This was pornographic in 1898, since rutting behaviors were acknowledged only in mammals lower on the evolutionary scale. In 1899, George Hamlin Fitch would chastise Norris in the *San Francisco Chronicle* for giving attention to the "odor femina" in his most genteel novel, *Blix*.[5]

Stretching the parameters of the genre in all directions, Norris next has Moran capture Hoang, the heroine torturing him in order to learn the location of the ambergris: she inserts a file in his mouth, binds his head so that his teeth are clenched, and then proceeds to work the file in and out. Ross has to leave the scene, the audible consequences are so gruesome. With Hoang soon lisping the information desired, only a full-scale battle with the pirates remains. In this primitive order of experience, Ross completes his break from the ethos of salted almonds and finger sandwiches. He is fully initiated into manhood as he observes his victim writhing on the ground at his feet: "The knowledge that he could kill filled him with a sense of power that was veritably royal. . . . It was the joy of battle, the horrid exhilaration of killing, the animal of the race, the human brute suddenly aroused and dominating . . . centuries of civilization" (*M*, 215).

In battle, Moran too becomes a homicidal creature. The emergence of a primitive personality within her as well has occurred, and from racial memory come words and snatches of sagas in Old Norse. In a frenzy, she has "lapsed back to the Vikings and sea-rovers of the tenth century . . . deaf to all reason" (*M*, 216). And thus does Norris complete his portrait of human nature – male *and* female – denying the exalted concept of humanity preferred by Victorians. Ross enjoys killing as much as book buyers enjoy vicarious participation in the same; Moran is wholly out of control, positioned to thrill the romance reader even more.

Love: Predator and Prey

The struggle with the pirates is already settled, but Moran is still in her battle fever and attacks Ross with her dirk uplifted. It is here that Norris most clearly signals the parodic intention that has alternated with his desire to succeed in the creation of a successful adventure tale, for this surprisingly proves to be the grand, long-expected love scene. Offered is the inverted equivalent of the balcony scenes in Shakespeare's *Romeo and Juliet* and Gounod's opera *Faust*, as love blossoms on the beach amidst Chinese corpses, and Moran, struggling to kill Ross, finally learns what it means to be like Josie Herrick, a member of the "weaker sex."

When Moran, literally berserk, attacks him, he at first tries to subdue her. But her fury increases, and he realizes that he is fighting for his life. His newfound strength proves the equal of Moran's, and they strike each other, blow for blow. When he sees his chance, he "plant[s] his knuckles squarely between her eyes where her frown was knotted hard, hoping to stun her and end the fight once and for all" (*M*, 219). This fails. His next strategy is more successful: "Wilbur met her half-way, caught her round the neck and under the arm, gripping her left wrist with his right hand behind her; then, exerting every ounce of strength he yet retained, he thrust her down and from him, until at length, using his hip as a pivot, he swung her off her feet, threw her fairly on her back, and held her so, one knee upon her chest, his hands closed vise-like on her wrists" (*M*, 220). This tableau surely merits treatment from an illustrator, which it so far has not received.

With Ross's knee on her chest and her forehead beginning to swell, Moran comes to her senses. Ross's unique courtship display has worked: " 'I'm the weaker of us two, and that's a fact. You've beaten, mate – I admit it; you've conquered me, and,' she continued, smiling again and shaking him by the shoulder, – 'and, mate, do you know, I love you for it' " (*M*, 221). She then transmutes into a clinging-vine female recalling Yvernelle and soon proves absolutely dependent on Ross. He has become a man; Moran, her brutally powerful personality extirpated by ennobling love, has approached as closely as she can the kind of woman normally found in popular romances. It "was no longer Moran who took the initiative – who was the leader. The brief fight upon the shore had changed all that" (*M*, 222).

An End to the Fantastic Voyage

In mid-March 1898, while still writing in New York against his deadlines at *The Wave*, Norris had to discover a way to execute the dénouement and finale. On 12 March, he wrote to a bluestocking friend in San Francisco, Elizabeth H. Davenport, that he was hard pressed by his "hammer and tongs work" for the McClure syndicate and *McClure's Magazine*. He was of "two minds" about how to conclude the *Moran* project (*Letters*, 47): Should Moran be killed or go filibustering in Cuba with Wilbur? He chose the former option. After a brief stop at Coronado Beach's Hotel del Coronado, Ross and Moran drop anchor in San Francisco Bay where she is stabbed to death by the insidious Hoang. Hoang disappears into Chinatown with the ambergris. The *Bertha Millner*, with Moran sprawled on her deck, is swept out to the Pacific before Ross's eyes, "a speck that dwindled and dwindled, then slowly melted away into the gray of the horizon." It is a grand romantic finale equalling Poe's and Gabriele D'Annunzio's conflations of eroticism and mortality as Moran returns whence she came, "out to the world of romance": "The schooner swept by, shot like an arrow through the swirling currents of the Golden Gate, and dipped and bowed and courtesied to the Pacific that reached toward her his myriad curling fingers. They enfolded her, held her close, and drew her swiftly, swiftly out to the great heaving bosom, tumultuous and beating in its mighty joy, its savage exultation of possession" (*M*, 291-92). As with all works truly related to the Romantic Love tradition, it is essential that the great love *not* be consummated. Beginning with the proper formula, *Moran* ends in the proper fashion, with Ross pining for the joy that is never to be.

Moran Viewed Seriously

Given what occurs between the beginning and the end, *Moran* finally defies the application of any one description of its character.[6] It is indeed an adventure-romance, a pragmatic response to market-place realities in early 1898 that met the standard against which John Phillips at the S. S. McClure syndicate judged it. It is a serious piece of fiction in that sense, and there is no need to defend before critics such literature which has as its chief function the entertainment of an adventure-hungry readership. It is also a work that Norris, at moments of especially vigorous plot development and scenic description, appears to have enjoyed writing. As we can see in an 1898 *Wave* tale of a sailor who falls in love with a drowned girl, "The Drowned Who Do Not Die,"[7] Norris could be "carried away" by a truly exotic conceit just as Howells, of all people, could confess to having read *Moran* with "breathlessness."[8] But another and more decadent authorial personality is disclosed by the sardonic delight he took in outrageously pillorying the adventure-romance genre and the Josie Herrick-like readership addicted to sensation piled on sensation. This is especially clear when Norris takes Josie Herrick backstage to meet the star of the melodrama. On the filthy deck of the *Bertha Millner*, Josie – like many a reader – does not know quite how to respond to this heroine before her, as shocked as Norris intended she should be: "It was long before the picture left Wilbur's imagination. Josie Herrick, petite, gowned in white, crisp from her maid's grooming; and Moran, sea-rover and daughter of an hundred Vikings, towering above her, booted and belted, gravely clasping Josie's hand in her own huge fist"(*M*, 266-67).

One other perspective requires comment when Ross Wilbur's initiation into manhood is viewed in light of *bildungsromane* like *Vandover* and *Blix*, or the stories of Annixter's and Laura's maturations in *The Octopus* and *The Pit*. While *Moran* concludes without an answer to the question of what Ross himself will do with his life, it is clear that Norris was giving thought to the question of maturation itself during the course of the novel. Ross's rite-of-passage experience in Magdalena Bay clearly defies the civilized values that Norris knew because it involves a regression to a barbaric condition requisite for survival in the tooth-and-claw environment in which Norris places his hero. The *Literary World* reviewer observed the wisdom of "killing off" Moran; how could a woman with her values, not to mention her appearance, ever fit into Ross Wilbur's world?[9] But what of Ross himself? In what way will he now fit into quotidian life of 1898? At the beginning of his tale he is one of San Francisco's *jeunesse dorée* often lampooned in *The Wave* – a "Brownie," as the uninitiated were then termed. As surely as the values that prevail at sea are different from those that prevail on land in Crane's "The Open Boat" (1897), those conditions under which Ross assumed manhood are not transferable, or even relevant, to life in San Francisco as he knows it.

Or are they? Is regression to primitive instincts or a degree of brutality requisite for a life well lived? There is some truth in Moran's assertion that "the strongest of us are going to live and the weakest are going to die" (*M*, 191). Perhaps there is something of positive value in the instincts that finally surface in the once-mincing devoté of stuffed olives that was Ross Wilbur. Is there a *via media* between effeteness and savagery that Norris had in mind? *Moran* does not provide an answer. It simply ends, leaving the question of maturation up in the air – either as surely as does *The Adventures of Huckleberry Finn* (1884) or as ambiguously as does *The Red Badge of Courage* (1895).

Moran was hardly Norris's last or clearest word on how one discovers the way things are and makes the requisite adjustments in order to survive and flourish. It was hardly his closest examination of "reality," although at the same time it was more than the bit of mere kite flying he told Howells it was.

Chapter Three

McTeague

When the serialization of *Moran* in *The Wave* ended on 8 April 1898, Norris had been in the employ of S. S. McClure in New York for nearly two months. He was mainly engaged in editorial activities, it seems, for neither *McClure's Magazine* nor the newspaper clients of the McClure syndicate then published anything by him. In late April, however, the Spanish-American War provided new opportunities. McClure sent Norris to report from Key West. Stalled there for what the journalists termed the war's "rocking-chair" phase, he finally got to Cuba in June and had the chance to describe the action. But when he returned to New York in early August, not one word of his had been printed – as far as we now know. Two Cuban articles, *"Comida"* and "With Lawton at El Caney," were not published until March and June 1899.[1] Seriously ill with malaria, Norris went to San Francisco to recuperate until October.

Norris returned to New York in a positive mood. The success of *Moran*, published in September 1898, had made Doubleday & McClure Co. amenable to the publication of *McTeague*, and in February 1899, he saw the appearance of the text he had been developing since he was a senior at Berkeley. The idea for the novel had come from the newspapers. On 10 October 1893, the San Francisco *Examiner* reported that an alcoholic "brute named Patrick Collins stabbed his wife to death in the Felix Adler Free Kindergarten yesterday morning." He had killed her "because she would not give him money and would not live with him."[2] During the 1894-95 academic year Norris spent at Harvard, sections of the novel were in process; by the fall of 1897 it was essentially completed at the Big Dipper gold mine in the Sierra Nevadas, east of Colfax, California (*Letters*, 109).

The Zolaesque Framework for *McTeague*

Like Emile Zola's *L'Assommoir*, *McTeague* concerns the rise and fall
of an individual. Zola's physically handicapped Gervaise Coupeau
struggles up from the lower classes, overcoming seemingly insupera-
ble obstacles to enter the world of the *petit bourgeois* as the owner
of her own laundry. *McTeague* is a similar success story for half its
length, as the hero experiences upward mobility, transcending the
limitations of both his low intelligence and humble origins. Because
of the aid of a wife given to impeccable housekeeping and financial
management, his own dutiful performance in his largely self-taught
profession of dentistry, and the extraordinary good fortune of Mrs.
McTeague having won $5,000 in a lottery, he has come to taste plea-
sures of American life not known to his parents. Mac, the son of a
lowly Irishman at a time when the Irish were viewed as an inferior
breed, is the kind of individual one might point to when celebrating
the American Dream. That his wife, Trina, seems a bit unstable appears the only truly unmanageable problem with which he has to
deal at the midpoint of his story. The novel ends in the nightmarish
way *L'Assommoir* does, though. Mac is handcuffed to a corpse in the
middle of Death Valley, after he has beaten his wife to death
following the painful descent of both into economic ruin and psy-
chopathologies that, nearly a century later, still appear unnervingly
bizarre. *McTeague* represents a particular type of Naturalistic fiction
(or Zolaesque Romanticism): the novel of degeneration.

Norris's multifaceted masterpiece has been interpreted in various ways. A major emphasis has been that *McTeague*, like
L'Assommoir, illustrates how characters' lives are shaped positively
and negatively not only by the exercise of free will but by the deter-
mining influences of heredity and environment. Another is that, as in
Zola's *La Bête Humaine* (1890) and an American novel that Norris
described as Naturalistic, James Lane Allen's *A Summer in Arcady*
(1896),[3] *McTeague* is a critical reaction to contemporaneous idealism regarding man as a noble creature superior to others in the
instinct-governed animal kingdom. Allen pictured two young lovers
as becoming sexually aroused, describing this as simply a natural development, and Norris approved of this unconventional acknowl-
edgment that the hero and heroine, without shame, had this in
common with dumb brutes. To his mind, it was time to admit the

truth with regard to man as a sexually driven creature like the beasts of the field and to do away with the notion that arousal per se must result in guilt and self-recrimination. Like *Moran*, *McTeague* focuses on a different kind of "brutality" in man – the brutality luridly described in Zola's portrait of the "human beast": a sometimes violently predatory creature in whom, despite the preachments of Victorian moralists, the amoral traits that ensured the evolutionary survival of the fittest dominate. Furthermore, as did Zola, Norris focused on what both Victorians and anti-Victorians might agree is truly abnormal or pathological in human behavior, attempting a more "scientific" explanation of the genetic and environmental causes than those offered by moralists who tended to explain aberration as merely a personal failure in self-control. Norris saw the probable causes of the neurotic and psychotic as multiple and complex, and *McTeague* is a correspondingly complex work, particularly in its portrait of Trina.

The Human Animal

It is not many paragraphs before Norris seems to echo Darwin's denial of modern man's special position at the apex of all creation. Evolutionarily viewed, man is described in chapter 1 as not so far removed from his caveman ancestors as Victorians liked to think: Mac immediately suggests something of the Neanderthal. His dental parlor on the lower middle-class Polk Street is hardly a cave, but as we learn how he passes the afternoon every Sunday we are prompted to see it thus. Following a gross feeding on "thick gray soup," "heavy, underdone meat," and a "sort of suet pudding" at a cheap restaurant, he returns to his lair to lie on his back "while his food digested." He is "crop-full, stupid, and warm" as he gradually falls asleep.[4] Waking, he routinely plays six lugubrious airs on his concertina. This inevitably brings to mind the days of his youth at the Big Dipper Mine where he was a common laborer for years, "trundling the heavy cars of ore in and out of the tunnel under the direction of his father," before his fiery, ambitious mother apprenticed him to an itinerant dentist (*Mc*, 2). The environment is now different, but Mac's appearance squares with his origins: "McTeague was a young giant, carrying his huge shock of blond hair six feet

three inches from the ground; moving his immense limbs, heavy with
ropes of muscle, slowly, ponderously. His hands were enormous,
red, and covered with a fell of stiff yellow hair; they were hard as
wooden mallets, strong as vises, the hands of the old-time car-boy.
Often he dispensed with forceps and extracted a refractory tooth
with his thumb and finger. His head was square-cut, angular; the jaw
salient, like that of the carnivora" (*Mc*, 3).

Mac's mind conforms to the physical type: even when not groggy
from the effects of an especially fatty meal, it proves "heavy, slow to
act, sluggish." When his friend Marcus Schouler talks political economy with him this Sunday afternoon, we find that simple concepts
such as "capital" and "labor" are beyond Mac, and that conversation per se is ludicrously difficult.[5] It takes him an inordinate amount
of time to respond to an idea that he does grasp. He is usually a few
sentences behind in the dialogue.

Still, Mac is an inoffensive, likable simpleton. Unlike the egotisti-
cal Marcus who, recalling *Moran*'s Captain Kitchell, is moved to violence by the merest suggestion of an affront, Mac is placid: "there
was nothing vicious about the man. Altogether he suggested the
draught horse, immensely strong, stupid, docile, obedient." Furthermore, his uncomplicated routines suggest near-idyllic contentment: "he felt that his life was a success, that he could hope for
nothing better" (*Mc*, 3).

Norris, however, has already made a brief reference to a socially-
and self-destructive genetic determinant that will, much later, render
him as vitriolic as Marcus and, later still, more sadistically "vicious."
At present, though, it appears irrelevant that, every "other Sunday
[his father] became an irresponsible animal, a beast, a brute, crazy
with alcohol" (*Mc*, 2). In the immediately succeeding chapters, Mac
appears to be more like his mother – an achievement-oriented fellow
soon looking forward to the day he will be able to upgrade his establishment via the advertisement of an enormous gilt molar outside
the parlor windows and – more personally – to win the hand of the
inestimable Trina Sieppe.

Sexuality and the Victorian Male

Trina enters Mac's life in chapter 2, when her cousin, Marcus, brings
her in for dental work. Although he is in his twenties, Mac has had
no intimate experience with women and is uneasy in her presence:
"He was embarrassed, troubled. These young girls disturbed and
perplexed him. He did not like them, obstinately cherishing that intuitive suspicion of all things feminine – the perverse dislike of an
over-grown boy" (*Mc*, 23). His ignorance of women, however, does
not spell naiveté about sexuality. This appears the one area in which
Mac is somewhat capable of conventional abstract reasoning;
indeed, when one day viewing the anesthetized Trina in his dental
chair, his initial experience of arousal reveals that he has learned to
make crude applications of metaphysical concepts such as "good"
and "evil" – although he cannot, of course, clearly define and com-
municate them. His attitude toward the "evil" of sex – his instincts
for which he never comes to understand – is central to the theme of
McTeague. Thus it falls on Norris to articulate Mac's classically Victorian reaction, which he does in the moralistic terms and images
popular in the mid-1890s via the narrative method of free indirect
discourse. As did Zola, Stephen Crane, and many other of Norris's
contemporaries before the stream-of-consciousness technique became a popular means of psychological revelation, Norris continues
to use the third-person singular but – without announcing the
shift – modulates his voice to describe his character's point of view
rather than his own. We learn just how conventional Mac is as the
considerably less prudish Norris adjusts the narrative voice to reveal
the psychological dimensions of the sinful ordeal through which the
dim-witted and largely inarticulate hero passes.

Having administered ether to Trina, Mac stares at her as she lies
there "unconscious and helpless, and very pretty. He was alone with
her, and she was absolutely without defense." Suddenly, Mac feels
the promptings of nature: "the animal in the man stirred and woke;
the evil instincts that in him were so close to the surface leaped to
life, shouting and clamoring" (*Mc*, 30). As the "fury in him" becomes
like that of "a young bull in the heat of high summer" (*Mc*, 31), one
may wonder what is so "evil" about this natural occurrence in a
creature whose sexual drive is as predictable as that in a young bull
at a certain season. But, again, this is the 1890s, and the genetically

determined development common to humanity at large becomes for Mac a moral crisis whose meaning is culturally predetermined by the then-commonplace notion that sex-related instincts, and all similarly brutelike drives, are sui generis "evil."

Thus begins Mac's battle with the sinful beast awakened at last: "Within him, a certain second self, another better McTeague rose with the brute; both were strong. . . . The two were at grapples. . . . It was the old battle, old as the world, wide as the world – the sudden panther leap of the animal, lips drawn, fangs aflash, hideous, monstrous, not to be resisted, and the simultaneous arousing of the other man, the better self that cries, 'Down, down,' without knowing why; that grips the monster; that fights to strangle it, to thrust it down and back" (*Mc*, 30). The "better self" loses to the "panther," and Mac does the dirty deed – *he kisses Trina once*. Ironically, this is the anticlimactic issue of this tremendous struggle between the forces of darkness and light. What is traumatic for the Victorian is comic for the author prone to take a satirical view of how old-style morality is as strong a determinism as sexual instinct.[6] In fact, one finds that Mac is gripped more by conscience than libido, for the seriocomic melodrama continues in a predictable manner as shame overwhelms him.

There follows an hysterical reaction to the tragic loss of innocence and the triumph of the vile brute "now at last alive, awake. . . . Ah, the pity of it! Why could he not always love her purely, cleanly? What was this perverse, vicious thing that lived within him, knitted to his flesh?" (*Mc*, 32). For moralistic Mac and the like-minded reader, "it" is more than merely the activation of a long-latent predisposition in a postpubescent male. As Trina recovers consciousness unaware of what has transpired, the guilt-bedeviled gentleman immediately does "the right thing": on the very afternoon of his first kiss, he makes his first marriage proposal, and this peculiar romantic scene describing the emergence of lust-quickly-become-love ends with the fair maiden vomiting before her wooer. The waggish Norris who had written for *The Wave* a similarly comic vignette of a coal-heaver being aroused by a washerwoman at work – and moved to an immediate marriage proposal – had this in common with Zola:[7] the *serious* work of art need not necessarily exclude the risible dimensions of its characters' experiences, as in chapter 3 of *L'Assommoir*. The consequences of brutal behavior can appear as silly as they may be somber.

Two quite serious points are, however, developed. First, Mac demonstrates that there is, indeed, an undeniably animalistic side to his nature and that the natural promptings of instinct may sometimes prove nearly irresistible (nearly, in that he does not wholly surrender to the urge). At the same time, Mac is not a brute *instead of* a human being: the "foul stream" of "evil" disclosed is not "heredity" in a Mac-specific sense. The brute is – or is in – man per se, as Norris makes clear when continuing his approximation of the Victorian mental-emotional crisis following the kiss: "The vices and sins of his father and of his father's father, to the third and fourth and five hundredth generation, tainted him. The evil of an entire race flowed in his veins. Why should it be? Was he to blame?" The "race" is not the shanty Irish but the human race; the sexual drive, the fury of the bull, "had faced him, as sooner or later it faces every child of man" (*Mc*, 32). No, Mac is not to blame for his randiness. And he is certainly not at fault when he remains chaste during his lengthy courtship of Trina through chapter 8.

A second theme initiated in chapter 2 is not apparent until much later when the multiple determinisms governing Mac's life become clear. Active sexual instincts need not eventuate in anything other than fornication – the satisfaction of the drive – unless one is culturally conditioned as the chaste hero is. His choices are sinful guilt on coitus before marriage or forbearance until afterwards, and he makes what appears the wiser choice at the time. What the reader finds, though, is that Mac thus steps into what proves both a biologically and culturally determined snare prefigured by the mousetrap that snaps shut when Trina informs her mother of her engagement (*Mc*, 86). Morally compelled to the altar in large part so that he may know carnal bliss without guilt, Mac unwittingly ties himself to a mate whose neuroses will contribute mightily to his degeneration.

Sexuality and the Victorian Female

Norris's fictional examination of the "sex problem" is extended to the female brute as well. She too is a Victorian youth with a strict set of values appropriate for the daughter of a man who is as explosively

violent as Marcus when anything within his ken does not conform to
his "Germanic" sense of order. Apparently having had to toe the
mark since the cradle because of Mr. Sieppe's sometimes blinding
rage for order, Trina is the ideal daughter. Unlike Mac, the ingénue is
not at all troubled by the presence of someone of the opposite sex.
She "was perfectly at her ease; doubtless the woman in her was not
yet awakened; she was yet, as one might say, without sex. She was
almost like a boy, frank, candid, unreserved" (*Mc*, 23). While the
administration of ether may be the cause of her vomiting before her
suitor, her terror over her first experience of a romantically aggressive male provides as likely an explanation. (The male hero of
Vandover and the Brute makes the same response when first in the
presence of a sexually vital female.) Her rough introduction to sexuality is more traumatic than Mac's, although she too is eventually
aroused.

With Marcus's help, Mac reinitiates his courtship in the socially
proper fashion. In chapter 5, he joins the Sieppe family for a picnic.
The pleasant day decides matters for them, and they date regularly.
Finally, Mac presses her in a more conventional manner for her
hand. When she again says no, the amorous predator seizes upon
the prey who proves much less resistant than the first time, and there
is more than a slight suggestion of a barnyard encounter during
mating season when Trina responds passionately: "Suddenly he took
her in his enormous arms, crushing down her struggle with his immense strength. Then Trina gave up, all in an instant, turning her
head to his. They kissed each other, grossly, full in the mouth." For
Mac, this is a new success: "I got her, by God!" he brags to himself.
For the Victorian female whose eroticism is expressed traditionally,
in active submission, the willful first surrender to the pleasure of a
lover's control has been bewildering: "Trina wrenched herself free
and drew back . . . her little chin quivering; her face, even to the
lobes of her pale ears, flushed scarlet; her narrow blue eyes brimming. Suddenly she put her head between her hands and began to
sob" (*Mc*, 84-85). When the mousetrap snaps, her being caught in
the sexual determinism leading to marriage is symbolized as well
(*Mc*, 86). In *McTeague*, women become as randy as men, governed
by the same "evil instinct." And so Trina and Mac move – or are
drawn – toward their wedding day, their progress accelerated when,

in chapter 7, they discover on returning from a vaudeville show at the Orpheum Theater that Trina has won the lottery.

The Intricate Logic of Multiple Determinisms

The life's complexity theme then begins to assume definition as three developments occur simultaneously over the next several chapters. First, Trina's good luck results in self-absorbed Marcus's ever-increasing rage over having given Mac permission to court his former sweetheart and thus having been deprived of the $5,000. In chapter 8, an inebriated Marcus throws his knife at Mac, barely missing him. That patched over to keep peace in the Sieppe clan, Marcus can barely control his anger at the McTeagues' wedding in the next chapter, sardonically belittling Mac whenever the opportunity presents itself. The two eventually have a violent confrontation, and Marcus's revenge proves fatal. But as this foreboding dimension of the novel is assuming shape, the second very different development is that the happy rise of the hero continues: he not only wins Trina but, as an engagement present from her, obtains his other major want. The gilt molar is hung outside the window of his prosperous dental parlor, a token of success and an advertisement promising even more. Under Trina's influence in their home environment, the cruder traits of the onetime miner disappear. By chapter 10, Mac is no longer eating with his knife and is changing his red-flannel underwear once a week and his linen shirts twice. He owns a high silk hat as the *Herr Doktor* of Polk Street should. He even appears to have risen to the level of sophistication of the politically minded Marcus, as is clear in this instance of free indirect discourse: "He commenced to have opinions, convictions – it was not fair to deprive tax-paying women of the privilege to vote; a university education should not be a prerequisite for admission to a dental college; the Catholic priests were to be restrained in their efforts to gain control of the public schools." Furthermore, Mac is becoming the most conventional of bourgeois daydreamers. He begins to entertain

> very vague, very confused ideas of something better – ideas for the most part
> borrowed from Trina. Some day, perhaps, he and his wife would have a house
> of their own. What a dream! A little home all to themselves, with six rooms
> and a bath, with a grass plat in front and calla-lilies. Then there would be

children. He would have a son, whose name would be Daniel, who would go
to High School, and perhaps turn out to be a prosperous plumber or house
painter. Then this son Daniel would marry a wife, and they would all live together in that six-room-and-bath house; Daniel would have little children.
McTeague would grow old among them all. The dentist saw himself as a ven-
erable patriarch surrounded by children and grandchildren. (*Mc*, 191-92)

The patrician narrator once again strikes the droll note, articulating
with tongue in cheek Mac's grand vision of a son with a high school
education who might rise to plumbing or house painting. But this is
the last time the lighthearted tone is heard in this novel.

As Mac enjoys his and Trina's idyllic vision of the future, the
third development in progress culminates in the first altercation between Mac and Trina a few pages later in chapter 10, when Mac
bungles a real-estate transaction. " 'Thirty-five dollars just thrown out
of the window,' cried Trina, her teeth clicking, every instinct of her
parsimony aroused" (*Mc*, 205). Like Marcus, she is enraged by the
loss of money. At this point in her life, Trina has something in common not only with Marcus but with the miserly junkman Zerkow who
lives in their neighborhood: all three become irrational when threatened with the losses of the kind just suffered. And genetic
determinants, according to the racial theory of the turn of the
century, account for the similarity among them: Zerkow is a Polish
Jew; Marcus Schouler is presumably German-Swiss because of his
kinship to Trina's family. Their racially inherited trait of acquisitiveness proves a primary factor in their deaths and the destruction they
leave in their wakes.

Trina: A Profound Study in Degeneracy

Trina receives her genetic coding in chapter 8, when her talent for
carving the animals in the Noah's Ark sets sold by her Uncle Oelber-
mann is explained: "Trina's ancestors on both sides were German-
Swiss, and some long-forgotten forefather of the sixteenth century,
some worsted-leggined wood-carver of the Tyrol, had handed down
the talent of the national industry, to reappear in this strangely dis-
torted guise" (*Mc*, 133). Along with that talent came another Swiss
trait: "Economy was her strong point. A good deal of peasant blood
still ran undiluted in her veins, and she had all the instinct of a hardy

and penurious mountain race – the instinct which saves without any thought, without idea of consequence – saving for the sake of saving, hoarding without knowing why" (*Mc*, 134). Unlike Mac's comparatively simple self-destructive genetic legacy, which is not activated until chapter 15, Trina's is triggered early. Shortly after the marriage, the signs of increasing niggardliness become apparent: "It was a passion for her to save money. . . . She did not save . . . for any ulterior purpose, she hoarded instinctively" (*Mc*, 188). By the time she hysterically lashes out at Mac for losing $35, it is clear, however, that more than Swiss ancestry is at work.

As Barbara Hochman most sensitively observes in *The Art of Frank Norris, Storyteller*, there is a Trina-specific psychological factor to be taken into account, generally describable as a free-floating sense of insecurity that manifests itself whenever the daughter of the ultraorganized and all-organizing Mr. Sieppe feels threatened by unpredictable developments or the – to her – chaos of sudden change.[8] She has a mania for external order and stability that compensates for the remarkably weak ego given its shape in a household where independence was not encouraged but conformity to her father's will was. The lottery prize is a cause of stress as well as a blessing, for she and not her father is suddenly responsible for its management: "it was only since her great winning in the lottery that she had become especially penurious. . . . Never, never, never should a penny of that miraculous fortune be spent; rather it should be added to" (*Mc*, 188). The security it promises is accompanied by the fear of losing the same; within six months she has replaced the $200 spent on her wedding. That she, rather than her father, pays for it suggests that the niggardly home environment reinforces her hoarding instinct.

When fear of her money diminishing is not the immediate focus, Trina acts as anxiously regarding another external source of security: Mac. During the engagement a "brusque outburst" of her affection is significantly phrased interrogatively: "Oh, Mac, do you truly, really love me – love me big?" (*Mc*, 135). Taking risks is dangerous; she has to be able to depend on him. When after the wedding she must part from the doting mother who then "rocked [her] in her arms as though she were a child again" (*Mc*, 177), Trina finds the loss traumatic. Finally overcoming the terror of being alone with her husband, she plaintively whispers that he must be good to her, "for you're all that I have in the world now" (*Mc*, 180). The mother's role is transferred to Mac by a young woman seemingly incapable of emotional autonomy. Trina's prenuptial "outbursts of affection" continue well into the marriage – with the same questions regarding Mac's reliability recurring: "He had come to submit to them good-naturedly, answering her passionate inquiries with a 'Sure, sure, Trina, sure I love you. What – what's the matter with you?'" (*Mc*, 189). What is the matter is that her neurotic clinging to money and to Mac is symptomatic of a profoundly dependent person who, leaving her parents, has reordered her life to replace the mental and emotional stabilizers that an anal-retentive child once enjoyed at home. To be deprived of either source of order spells disaster for one with no inner resource of self-reliance on which to draw. Given her Swiss heredity and its effects exacerbated by her neurosis, however, the worst loss would be that of her money. To protect it, she is finally willing to sacrifice her parents when they are in a financial crisis and to give up Mac.

The Complex Structure: Main Plot and Subplots

When what Trina perceives as economic ruination occurs, thanks to Marcus's compulsive need for revenge, the rise of the McTeagues abruptly halts, and the three just-described main plot developments coalesce. Chapter 10 closes with Trina sorry for being so mean to Mac about the $35 but unable to make amends by sharing the cost of the loss from her private savings: her compulsive "love of money" rises in her: "It's stronger than I" (*Mc*, 210-11). Marcus, *his* money "stolen" by Mac, suffers a final indignity from his onetime friend; Mac breaks his arm during a fight at a picnic in chapter 11. His revenge is reporting Mac to the authorities for practicing dentistry without a license, and it is the beginning of the end for the McTeagues as the notice to cease his practice arrives in chapter 12. Their furniture sold in chapter 13, they move into poorer quarters, and Mac cannot find permanent employment. The arch of the novel's design is now apparent as the downward turn in Mac's story occurs. As phrased at the beginning of chapter 15, "Then the grind began" (*Mc*, 284). *McTeague* now clearly becomes a tale of degeneration.

As the downward movement proceeds, the novel's two seemingly gratuitous subplots begin to reveal their thematic purpose. Throughout the work, the main plot has been punctuated with the comical comings and goings of two quirky, Dickensian characters, Old Grannis and Miss Baker, who – although apparently in their sixties – become lovers in a markedly preadolescent manner. It is the first love affair each has had, and Norris offers this analogy to the Mac-Trina relationship to reinforce the credibility of his peculiar representatives of the 1890s, male and female. As shy and as clumsy as Mac and Trina were, Grannis and Baker experience grand crises of embarrassment when in each other's presence. Eventually, they are able to launch a courtship. But, significantly, something is missing: sex. The simple innocence of the stereotypical hero and heroine in "nice," morally uplifting fictions is thus parodied by Norris as Grannis and Baker eventually become engaged, and pure love, untainted by nasty biological drives, flowers according to the script treasured by Victorian idealists. This subplot is satirically fashioned, then, as a counterpoint to the more realistic, decidedly anti-Victorian main plot in which not only sexual but other drives loom large. As we turn from Mac, the human brute, to Old Grannis, within whom the brute does not exist or has long-since atrophied, we ask, Which portrait of human nature is *truer* to the way things actually are? Because Mac and Trina become increasingly grotesque after chapter 14, their previous normalcy as implied by the first subplot is essential to the development of themes about human nature which are universal in their import.

The second subplot provides a third love story and, through the beginning of the McTeagues' decline in chapter 15, serves a function similar to that of the first subplot: by way of contrast, it even more powerfully enhances the image of Mac's and Trina's *relative* normalcy. Maria Macapa and Zerkow are a bit more eccentric than Grannis and Baker; indeed, they invite clinical diagnoses shortly after their first, precocious displays of mental instability and incipient idiocy. Mac is a genius compared to these two; Trina is a model of stability. Maria's tic – her need to announce that she once had a flying squirrel and let him go – is the curtain raiser; her most memorable aberration, though, is her oracular gift for sensuously describing a nonexistent gold table service that she believes her family once owned. Illiterate and delusional, she exhibits poetic brilliance when called on to articulate this fantasy. The local junkman, the red-headed Jew Zerkow, enters the story as one whose hereditary acquisitiveness has already been exaggerated to monstrously monomaniacal proportions in his feverish obsession with gold. He is as irresistibly drawn to Maria as Mac was to Trina – although not because of anything so normal as carnal appetite. Zerkow illustrates that the "evil instinct" of normal sexuality pales in its alleged malevolence when viewed alongside his delirious ecstasy over the gold service described by Maria. Maria's story – a pure piece of pornography for him – cannot be heard often enough. Zerkow thus defines the truly abnormal and even marries the repulsive charwoman so as to have at hand the means to satisfy his perverted sexuality.

The Maria-Zerkow tale serves other functions as well. Maria stands as a measure of degeneracy when Trina eventually descends to her level and then to the even lower condition of the increasingly insane Zerkow. Zerkow also gauges the irrationality of Marcus as he delusionally fixates on Trina's $5,000 as his and throws his knife at the man he believes has stolen it; *his* money is as real to Marcus as the nonexistent treasure is to the psychotic Zerkow, who, in chapter 16, cuts Maria's throat for having forgotten the story of the gold service and thus "stolen" it from him. Finally, Zerkow's condition foreshadows Mac's descent to the level of an homicidal maniac. What is astounding about the centrality of Zerkow to this picture of life is that, when he first appears, it is inconceivable that Mac, Trina, and Marcus could ever develop traits like his; what is thematically crucial about the fact that they do is that life is *that* unpredictable.

The Long Slide Downward

In chapters 13 through 15, Mac takes his first, unwitting steps toward identification with Zerkow. While still possessed of the respectable personality of the bourgeois, the loss of regular income is stressful because he has become used to the now-too-expensive life-style to which Trina introduced him. Surrendering the amenities for the sake of ready cash discomfits him in a more critical way, however: the things he loses are the proofs of his worth gathered since he came to San Francisco. He refuses to sell some, such as his canary and its cage, but the loss of his tokens of success spells failure. Depression and irritation become regular experiences exacerbated by criticisms from Trina: "I'm supporting you," she declares in chapter 14 (*Mc*, 273). Trina is for Mac both a passive reminder of his impotence and an active source of harassment, although Mac – despite a few outbursts over her cheapness – remains the essentially docile husband he has always been.

Trina unintentionally changes this in chapter 15. Her economies have become more extreme, and the possibility of adding another nickel to her hoard precipitates a new disaster. As Mac is leaving their wretched flat to search for work, Trina suspects that he has money and lies to him about having to buy heating oil and meal tickets:

> "Always after me about money," muttered the dentist; but he emptied his pockets for her, nevertheless.
>
> "I – you've taken it all," he grumbled. "Better leave me something for car fare. It's going to rain."
>
> "Pshaw! You can walk just as well as not. A big fellow like you 'fraid of a little walk; and it ain't going to rain." (*Mc*, 290)

It does rain. A cold drizzle chills him to the bone as he walks homeward without a job, reflecting on what he has suffered and blaming miserly Trina who has become "worse than old Zerkow" (*Mc*, 291). She does, after all, have her $5,000 invested with Uncle Oelbermann. Heise, a Polk Street shopkeeper, calls him into a saloon and treats him to whiskey for his health. The latent hereditary trait is activated: like his father, he becomes violent, threatening Trina when he returns home. Terrified, she quails before him; inebriated, he goes to sleep. After composing herself, Trina searches his pockets for change, unaware as chapter 15 ends that a "panther" that makes Mac's sexual drive look like a tabby has been unleashed within him.

Ambition wholly gone, Mac soon outdoes his father, who became a drunken "beast" only once a fortnight. In chapter 1, we are told that "there was nothing vicious about the man." Now the whiskey produces a "curious" effect, the emergence of Zola's *bête humaine*: "It did not make him drunk, it made him vicious. . . . [He] became, after the fourth glass, active, alert, quick-witted, even talkative; a certain wickedness stirred in him; . . . he found a certain pleasure in annoying and exasperating Trina, even in abusing her and hurting her" (*Mc*, 305). The sadistic turn becomes more pronounced as Mac adds to his repertoire in wife beating: he takes to biting Trina's fingers, "crunching and grinding them with his immense teeth, always ingenious enough to remember which were the sorest" (*Mc*, 309).

Meanwhile, Trina's relationship with her money is becoming as bizarre as the marriage to Mac. She locks the door, plays with the coins, burying her face in them, savoring their scent: "She even put the smaller gold pieces in her mouth, and jingled them there." Maria passionately describes imagined gold; as Trina sinks to the level of Maria, now her close friend, she speaks passionately *to* her beloved coins: "I love you so! All mine, every penny of it. . . . How I've slaved and worked for you! And I'm going to get more; I'm going to get more, more, more; a little every day" (*Mc*, 308). The coins have displaced Mac, although not completely. Trina will not surrender any possible source of security in her increasingly threatening life.

As Mac becomes a sadist, Trina makes the necessary adjustments, because losing him is unthinkable: in "some strange, inexplicable way this brutality made Trina all the more affectionate; aroused in her a morbid, unwholesome love of submission, a strange, unnatural pleasure in yielding, in surrendering herself to the will of an irresistible, virile power" (310). Sadly, there is a logic to this delight in surrendering for the sake of personally experiencing control in an otherwise uncontrollably worsening situation. Furthermore, it is not the first time security was had by submission: her love for Mac first manifested itself in a dramatic surrender that now seems tame; before Mac, security was had via the dictatorial control of Mr. Sieppe.

At this point in chapter 16, the congruence of the Zerkows and McTeagues is made clear: Maria and Trina talk at length about the skills of their sadistic husbands. The two connoisseurs in masochism "had long and excited arguments as to which were the most effective means of punishment" (*Mc*, 311). Maria cites the lash of a whip; Trina contends that the whip butt is the more injurious. The measure of the two is that neither is complaining – only taking pride in the bruises she displays.

The competitive but sisterly conversations soon cease as Zerkow, convinced that Maria has hidden the gold service in the tale she used to tell, kills her. Trina then suffers the same shock that Zerkow did when deprived of his imaginary gold; her real savings are stolen by Mac. She becomes delirious as her ultimate nightmare materializes: she loses both Mac and the money not invested with her uncle on the same day. Making matters even worse, the next morning she learns that she cannot continue her manufacture of Noah's Ark sets. That source of income disappears as a physician observes her chewed hand, which has become infected. Chapter 19 introduces Trina as a Maria-like charwoman in a kindergarten who has difficulty with her scrub brush because two of her fingers and her thumb have been amputated.

An End to Madness

Trina's life has reached its nadir: its only bright spot is the lottery money she has retrieved in gold pieces from her uncle. It is the center of *her* life, and Zerkow's psychosexual relationship with gold is now hers: "One evening she had . . . spread all the gold pieces between the sheets, and had then gone to bed, stripping herself, and had slept all night upon the money, taking a strange and ecstatic pleasure in the touch of the smooth flat pieces the length of her entire body" (*Mc*, 361). Her lovers, and her life, are next taken from her by Mac, whom Trina rebuffs when he returns penniless for aid. Driven by rage, he beats her to death and flees San Francisco with the sack of gold coins. The brute-become-bestial returns to his erstwhile lair – the mining country in the Sierra Nevadas. It is a primitive environment suitable for the onetime Victorian who has shed all traces of his civilized self.

Marcus soon in pursuit to retrieve *his* gold coins, the predatory Mac becomes prey, developing the trait distinguishing animals in the latter category: acute attentiveness. It is here that Norris qua Romantic shows his hand with the extravagant notion that a "sixth sense" can alert Mac to the threat still miles away, before which he flees. In 1899, however, the sixth sense phenomenon was not so dubious a thing as it now appears; Arthur Conan Doyle, William James, and William Butler Yeats were among the many sophisticated contemporaries interested in psychical research and phenomena of the kind. San Francisco was a mecca for such like-minded individuals as Norris's friends Gelett Burgess and Bruce Porter. Still, despite Mac's newly activated "instinct," Marcus apprehends him in Death Valley – but only to know the outcome of Zerkow's and Trina's mania for gold. Having lost their water owing to an accident, neither Mac nor he can survive. It is a mercy that Mac kills him. As the novel ends, Mac discovers that Marcus had handcuffed them together during their final battle: "McTeague remained stupidly looking around him, now at the distant horizon, now at the ground, now at the half-dead canary chittering feebly in his little gilt prison" (*Mc*, 442). Fittingly, images of bewilderment and helplessness close Mac's story.

McTeague's Themes: Uncertainties Clarified but Not Eliminated

The reader, of course, does not at this point share the sense of total confusion and impotence suggested here. Like Norris, he or she enjoys the satisfaction that comes with an understanding of how heredity and environment, working hand in hand, determine the courses of the characters' lives. Indeed, viewing the novel from the vantage point of the last page and tracing out the main lines of development, it seems that a relatively simple cause-and-effect exercise in a necessitarian logic has been completed. Such, at least, is a popular description of the main plot and theme offered by critical commentators[9]; in fact, this description is consistent with one point of view employed by Norris as he meets one of Aristotle's criteria for great art: the reader obtains intellectual clarification regarding the perplexing nature of human experience. *McTeague* does appear to reduce life to intellectually manageable proportions, even to simple formulae. Readers with Trina's orientation to life will appreciate that.

A second point of view is developed throughout the novel, however. While *Moran* was ambiguous, *McTeague* is an ambivalent work in which the pellucid certainties made possible by a deterministic philosophy stand in a dialectical relationship with the murky uncertainties encountered by the characters themselves. To clarify what transpires and grasp its significance in retrospect is not to forget or explain away the confusing twists in human experience that are pictured. Our understanding of the forces at work in *McTeague* – or *Othello* – does not obviate the sensitively rendered fact about the *immediate* experience of life had by the characters who are participants, rather than spectators: as also happens in real life, and to individuals of much greater wisdom than the cast of characters assembled here, the flow of events is overwhelming. As with Aristotelian tragedy, understanding *follows* the experience of pity and fear. It does not negate the original cause for pitying the characters whose lives are out of control or the reason for fearing that one's life may become as threateningly confusing as those of the characters.

In *McTeague*, Norris speaks with certainty about the meaning of events. But the novel requires that one note as well the thematic and autobiographical significance of the kind of experience he chose to picture. Like Darwin's *Origin of Species* (1859), *McTeague* offers a rationally satisfying, post-Victorian paradigm that demonstrates how things came to be the way they are. But, also like *Origin*, it does not in consequence eliminate the instability and unpredictability of a biological world in which chance developments are as significant as genetic and environmental determinants. "Coincidences" abound in *McTeague*, and they are not only a means to effective storytelling; they are thematically significant for a writer whose keen sense of the uncertain nature of life is as prominent as his obvious desire to provide a meaningfully coherent explanation.

Chapter Four

Vandover and the Brute

While *Vandover and the Brute* was not published until 1914, almost 12 years after Frank Norris's death, the conception of its hero was available by 1892, when a rakish Vandover appeared in "The Way of the World." Norris was, it seems, developing the manuscript in earnest during the 1894-95 academic year he spent at Harvard, submitting *Vandover*-related themes for the writing course he was then taking. When he completed the bulk of the story, however, is moot. One infers that it was not published in his lifetime for two reasons. First, it was too graphic in its description of the unmentionables of Victorian life. As late as 1913, his mother was still reluctant to allow his brother, Charles, to arrange for its appearance.[1] Second, although the manuscript was considered by his American and English publishers in 1899, Norris seems never to have finished the novel to his satisfaction. When Grant Richards received it from the London representative of Doubleday & McClure Co., Norris wrote him from New York on 27 November 1899 and actually discouraged its acceptance by noting that it was "hardly available for any publisher just yet" (*Letters*, 94). When Charles later edited the now-lost manuscript, it appears not to have been more finished: as he told Franklin Walker, he not only deleted what he considered offensive elements but added approximately 5,000 words before it was ready for submission to Doubleday, Page & Co. Even then, Charles did not think highly of the novel, and the publicity for it played on the idea that it represented incomplete apprentice-work produced at the same time as *McTeague*.

That *Vandover* was mainly written during the same period as *McTeague* is also apparent in the preoccupations of a young writer ruminating on his adolescence in both works: the sexual instinct did not again loom so large in his novels. Whatever the trauma that may have attended Norris's own experience in this regard, he seems to

have largely satisfied in *Vandover* the need to protest the trying ordeal through which young Victorians reared in proper circumstances
like his own had to pass. While other topics receive attention,
Vandover is primarily an angry response to the idealistic, or unrealis-
tic, status quo notions about human sexuality to which his genteel
culture had introduced him.

Vandover's Design: Another "Novel of Degeneration"

Vandover is more overtly autobiographical than *McTeague* and in
many respects represents Norris's imagined scenario for how his life
might have turned out. The hero is not a crude miner who became
an unlicensed dentist in one of the humbler neighborhoods of San
Francisco. He is from Norris's own upper middle-class background.
Like B. F Norris, Van's father pays for art instruction and a university
education; like Norris, Van initiates a desultory career as a painter
and does not have to hold a job since income is not a consideration.
He has a dilettante's social life and is informally engaged to a bona
fide lady – such as those with whom Norris himself associated in
beau monde San Francisco – a genteel vessel of purity named Turner
Ravis. At a higher socioeconomic and cultural level, Van types the
good life more splendiferously than Mac. Just as suddenly, however,
Van's downward spiral begins.

He seduces a less ladylike young woman named Ida Wade. The
consequence for Ida is her suicide; for Van it is twofold: he loses his
father – whose heart could not stand the stress of Van's fatally un-
wise philandering – and, when his culpability becomes public
gossip, is driven from the comfortable high society to which he has
well adapted himself as a man of leisure. On his own as a social
pariah and without the father who cared for his needs and wants,
Van bears a resemblance to Trina McTeague in that, when the exter-
nally available sources of order in his life are removed, he proves incapable of changing from a dependent person to a positively self-
reliant one. The need for independent thought and action spells
crisis for him.

An old friend who made all of Van's decisions for him during
their student years at Harvard has become an attorney, and he pre-

tends to come to Van's aid when Ida Wade's father sues for his daughter's death. Lazy and imperceptive, Van is easily victimized by Charlie Geary: this unscrupulous predator with a relentless survival-of-the-fittest orientation is representing Mr. Wade as well. His estate diminished but still sufficient for his wants, Van self-indulgently tri-fles away his time, when he is not energetically whoring, drinking, and gambling. Syphilis compounds his problems physiologically; guilt in the reckless sinner plagued by a Victorian conscience works its psychological effects. Hallucinating a wolflike monster that has grown large within him and devoured all of the good in his charac-ter, he experiences psychotic episodes in which he acts like the beast he believes he has become, uncontrollably growling and barking. As his tale ends, he is like Trina scrubbing the kindergarten floors, for the now-penniless Harvard graduate cleans rental cottages for Charlie.

As in *McTeague*, the question is, *How* did the hero arrive at this condition? Norris again focuses the reader's attention on the data of cause and effect. In this novel, however, genetic inheritance plays a lesser role. The influence of the environment in which Van was reared, flourished for a while, and degenerated is paramount.

An Experiment in Narrative Technique

The narrative of Van's life begins in an experimental manner, with Norris describing how mental debilitation has affected Van's adulthood before turning to Van's earliest years and the causes of this debilitation.[2] Thus, Van's mind after it is degenerate is the focus on the first page: "It was always a matter of wonder to Vandover that he was able to recall so little of his past life."[3] The weakness of memory in question is extraordinary: "With the exception of the most recent events he could remember nothing connectedly. What he at first imagined to be the story of his life, on closer inspection turned out to be but a few disconnected incidents that his memory had preserved with the greatest capriciousness, absolutely indepen-dent of their importance" (*V*, 3). Van's earliest memory is that of his mother dying in a busy train station when he was eight: "her face became the face of an imbecile. . . . Her head rolled forward as though she were nodding in her sleep, while a long drip of saliva trailed from her lower lip" (*V*, 5).

Van's years between 8 and 13 are a blank, however, and what transpired immediately thereafter is difficult to determine: "In order to get at his life during his teens, Vandover *would have been obliged* to collect these scattered memory pictures as best he could, rearrange them in some more orderly sequence, piece out what he could imperfectly recall and fill in the many gaps by mere guess work and conjecture" (*V*, 5; italics added). Well before the end of the novel we realize why Norris is using the conditional mode here. These "scattered memory pictures" cannot be given coherent arrangement by the enfeebled hero recalling past events any more than Mac could clearly conceptualize or articulate his moral crisis before the anesthetized Trina. Van cannot accomplish what he "would have been obliged" to do to effect a sequential record of the crucial events of his adolescence. Norris must do this for the reader, filling in the gaps by means of speculation and using both conventional description and free indirect discourse to describe Van's consciousness.[4] He begins by turning back the clock to the summer of 1880 when Van was eight (*V*, 5), and the chronologically arranged pattern that develops is one expected from a Literary Naturalist: the reader is shown how Van's character, shaped by his environment, predisposed him to precipitate his own decline. The reader is also invited to participate in the reconstruction of the life as he notes that Van's understandings of what transpires appear to be at odds with events suggesting different interpretations.[5]

Life's Ironies

The ferocious womanizer in his twenties who makes the tremendous mistake of treating Ida Wade the way he does was, ironically, a virtuous boy in his teens who first discovered the mechanisms of procreation as loathsomely evil: "It was during Vandover's first year at the High School that his eyes were opened and that he acquired the knowledge of good and evil" (*V*, 9) – that is, the knowledge of sex, in the euphemistic Victorianism derived from the biblical story of Adam and Eve. While neither fornication nor even the desire for sexual experience was Eve's and Adam's sin, the "knowledge of good and evil" obtained by eating the forbidden fruit is immediately related by the censorious, proto-Victorian authors of Genesis to human sexuality. Fallen man's first emotional experience is shame for disobedience of God, and, strangely enough for modern readers, it manifests itself in Adam and Eve having to cover their unoffending genitals. Norris's own attitude toward this biblically fostered way of thinking about the human animal? His focus in the first chapter of *Vandover* is on the trauma induced by such an attitude toward sexuality and the long-term consequences for the hero. Thematically, the first chapter is heavily freighted.

As in *McTeague*, sex becomes a primary topic because of the unsolicited promptings of instinct. Van kept his "innocence" until very late, but "by and by he became very curious, stirred with a blind unreasoned instinct." In the Bible, "he came across a great many things that filled him with vague and strange ideas"; at his Episcopal church he notes for the first time the reference to the perils of childbirth in the prayer book's litany. Still, Van has formed no conceptions: "He puzzled over this for a long time, smelling out a mystery beneath the words, feeling the presence of something hidden, with the instinct of a young brute." At this point in *Vandover and the Brute*, the "brute" that is Van is morally neutral, emerging as neither good nor evil. The mystery he scents is indeed *hidden* in polite society, and before an idea of what it is forms, he receives an attitude-determining signal from his father: "He could get no satisfaction from his father and by and by began to be ashamed to ask him; why, he did not know." The event is a crucial one and a prime example of the psychological effects of environment. "It" is quickly associated with, and permanently remains tied to, shame.

Van's schoolmates are not so reticent as his proper father, and his curiosity is satisfied in a less than delicate manner. "At length one day he heard the terse and brutal truth," which squares with the promptings he has felt: "In an instant he believed it, some lower, animal intuition in him reiterating and confirming the fact" (*V*, 10). A crisis develops when he understands what it is toward which instinct inclines. In simple Freudian terms, the conscious ego finds clarification and confirmation of the effects produced by the instinctive drive originating in the unconscious side of his personality, the id. Unfortunately, the new data are in conflict with the Victorian images of goodness that reside in his conventional superego, the conscience that associates shame with procreation-related activities: "he hated to think that people were so low, so vile."

An "Obstetrics" article in an encyclopedia exacerbates this conflict: "It was the end of all his childish ideals, the destruction of all his first illusions. The whole of his rude little standard of morality was lowered immediately. Even his mother, whom he had always believed to be some kind of an angel, fell at once in his estimation. She could never be the same to him after this, never so sweet, so good and so pure as he had hitherto imagined her" (V, 10-11). It is, theoretically, possible for one to readjust his view of what is "sweet," "good," and "pure" – at some time during maturation modifying the notion that sexual activity and birthing preclude virtuousness. But Van proves for the first of many times that he is not particularly prone to revising simplistic conceptions in light of realities, and his priggish father neither encourages nor helps him to rethink his "rude little standard of morality." The Victorian father too, perhaps, associates asexual purity with goodness and the impurity of sexual activity with evil. If so, Van certainly becomes his father's son. The goodness-asexuality equation is henceforth a fixed idea.

At the same time, though, the shocking evil he has discovered is fascinating. While he knows what shame-free goodness is, he becomes obsessed with the vileness that tainted the memory of his hallowed mother, and the amoral instinct of a young brute is soon associated with evil satisfactions of which he craves greater knowledge. Thus Norris relates the development that "little by little the first taint crept in, the innate vice stirred in him, the brute began to make itself felt, and a multitude of perverse and vicious ideas commenced to buzz about him like a swarm of nasty flies" (V, 11). Hearing about whores – that is, "the blunt Anglo-Saxon word for a lost woman" – takes him past the mechanics of conception and the specifics of childbirth to another view of the purpose of sexual activity: forbidden pleasure. Vandover "soon became filled with an overwhelming curiosity, the eager evil curiosity of the schoolboy, the perverse craving of the knowledge of" not sexuality per se but "vice." This equation is psychologically all-important because Van never views sex as other than vicious: it is pleasurable and necessary but still a vice. Physiologically, this equation proves disastrous: Van will satisfy the impure craving only with potentially syphilitic women he views as "lost," and Norris thus positions the reader to see how a *mere* attitude developed in childhood eventuates years later in a primary cause of Van's degeneration.

Norris speculates that things might have been otherwise. The polarities of asexual goodness and sexual evil in Van's mind might have been eliminated had Van's everyday environment been different. If there had only been some women about him at this point in his life, Norris observes, they might have helped him "to see the world in the right light and to gauge things correctly." The prosaic realities of mothers, sisters, aunts, and cousins might have curbed his pornographic obsessions. These polarities, however, remain constant throughout Van's story, and the consequences of his attitude toward women include Ida Wade's suicide. How this eventuates is clarified in chapter 1 by one of Norris's finest uses of irony: "he might have been totally corrupted while in his earliest teens had it not been for another side of his character that began to develop at the same time" (*V*, 11).

"Saved" from the Brute

Van is not "totally corrupted" because he naturally inclines toward a kind of activity that, first, gives him something else to do beyond entertaining lurid sexual fantasies and, second, provides him with purer images of women that antipodally counter the salacious ones he has developed: a balance of sorts is struck. This second tendency or side of his nature is not associated with shame. To the contrary, its development is encouraged by his father (and, by extension, the Victorian ethos that ever celebrated the "uplifting" value of "culture"): "He seemed to be a born artist" (*V*, 11). It "was evident that he possessed the fundamental *afflatus* [creative spirit] that underlies all branches of art" (*V*, 12). Like the sexual instinct, the artistic instinct manifests itself spontaneously. On his own, Van makes clay modelings, picks out tunes on the piano, gives dramatic performances in the parlor, and writes little tales. He literally does what comes naturally – as hereditarily predisposed to creativity as he is biologically programmed for procreative activity. But, as with sex and birthing defined by the encyclopedia in his home library and further defined by his father's negative attitude, Van's conceptualization of art is soon determined for him by the Victorian values represented

in *A Home Book of Art* and by the positive response of his father to
his *copyings* of its contents. These pictures are idealizations of
women – the least noble of which are those of coquettes – and they
allow the "better self" of Van to exercise itself as he reproduces the
images and the idealistic concepts they represent.

Copying pictures and conforming to his father's and instructor's
expectations, he eventually produces his masterpiece entitled *Flora*.
It transcends all of his considerable, previous work on "ideal
'Heads' " (*V*, 13-14). If we reasonably assume the drawing to have
been inspired by the most famous Flora of all – the Neoplatonic
beauty featured in Botticelli's *La Primavera* – we will likely have an
accurate approximation of the degree of idealization of the "woman"
in question, who is actually a goddess. And it is noteworthy that Van
executes only the head rather than the whole body (interpretable as
pregnant) of this mythological fertility figure. Cropped as well are
Botticelli's other four women clothed only in diaphanous garments.
One would not find in *A Home Book of Art* the virtually naked
nymph pursued by Zephyr to the right of Flora or the sumptuous
Three Graces in sheer gowns who are dancing at left.

Saints versus Sluts

The irony is that Vandover escapes "total corruption" through art.
But the female fantasy figures with which he deals do not effect a
more realistic point of view on women or sex; they do not obviate a
bifurcated view of woman as *either* a pure creature *or* a lowly whore.
In the Victorian framework, of course, there is no in-between, and in
chapter 2 when Van has his first encounter with a real woman, a
"chippie" he meets while at Harvard, the by-then fully developed
maladjustment dramatically reveals itself: he begins to vomit when in
the woman's presence and must quickly excuse himself. (Recall
Trina's vomiting when she first experiences a romantically aggressive
male.) Three days later, Van manages to keep his gorge down when,
"moved by an unreasoned instinct," he has sexual intercourse with
her (*V*, 24). *Then* begins the most distinctive rhythm of his life as he
moves into his twenties. Once the evil brute-within is sated, it is time
to reassert his better self. Traumatized not by an idea but the actual
experience of female vileness, Van feels that he "could never again

look a pure woman in the face." From Cambridge, Massachusetts, he confesses to his father in San Francisco, "asking his forgiveness and reiterating his resolve to shun such a thing forever after" (*V*, 24-25).

On his return to San Francisco at age 22, however, Van becomes sexually active. His better self loses control as "this thing grew upon him until it mounted to a veritable passion" (*V*, 28). The "animal in him, the perverse evil brute, awoke and stirred," and he has intercourse a second time with a prostitute named Flossie (*V*, 29), whereupon the pattern first seen at Harvard recurs. The brute fed, the better self can reassert itself until the brute demands satisfaction again. Van consequently develops a rationalization allowing for the sating of the Dr. Jekyll and Mr. Hyde sides of his personality. His premise is, "Those men only were perverted who allowed themselves to be corrupted by such vice." He sees himself as uncorrupted as long as the better self remains the dominant personality: "only on rare occasions did he permit himself to gratify its demands, feeding its abominable hunger from that part of him which he knew to be the purest, the cleanest, and the best" (*V*, 29-30). Van displays a Manichean view of life: good versus evil, saintly women versus sluttish ones, his better self versus the brute – and with no intermediate states between these extremes.

Van, then, has elaborated on rather than eliminated the conflict experienced when he first learned the "terse and brutal truth" about the animalism of human nature. We also detect the first suggestion of a culturally derived determinism at work: Van is proving a thrall not only to the beast of Victorian iconography but to the ideal conception of himself that currently exercises an even stronger hold on him. No middle way is visible.

Two Personalities

The two Vans flourish for three years, and chapters 3 and 4 make clear the way in which the two personalities manifest themselves. Chapter 3 features the better self during a typical evening at the home of Turner Ravis where cards are played and polite jokes are cracked. It is a tame, orderly, pleasant scene; the most uproarious happening is a glass inexplicably and suddenly cracking. Tragedy in this effervescently playful milieu consists of Dolly Haight, one of

Van's gentlemen friends, cutting his lip on the glass. This is high life among the gilded youth of San Francisco, reminiscent of a church social. Chapter 4 takes the reader to the "other" San Francisco of the Imperial Café where Van is well known. There he consorts with a more vigorous female whose beauty renders Turner anemic in comparison: the prostitute Flossie. It is clear why Van finds vice so attractive and why the intensely moral Dolly does not respond when Flossie suddenly kisses him. Dolly is the truly pure male, the less "masculine" Victorian that Van would like to be but cannot. From glasses of beer at Turner's, Van turns to more potent drinks, revelling through the night with his obstreperous cronies who hardly resemble the polite figures seen a few hours before.

Van types the general phenomenon of Victorian hypocrisy as he leads his double life. Indeed, the "compromises" made necessary by high public moral standards are the subject of a discussion by Van and his pals in chapter 7 (V, 96-102). Tracing his career through chapter 7, we find that he and many other young San Franciscans of his class can frequent the brothel as well as the family parlor with impunity; this appears to be a popular arrangement, and it is even argued by Van that proper young ladies tacitly condone the notion of a future mate with "experience" (V, 99). Victorian hypocrisy aside, disease and scandal appear the only potential problems, although precautions can be taken by the intelligent.

Van proves not especially intelligent. We discover that he has misjudged Flossie's "clean" appearance: although she seems to "radiate health" (V, 52), much later in the novel we find that she has already infected Dolly with syphilis via the kiss on his cut lip and that Van has contracted the disease from her in the normal manner. Van's lack of acumen is obvious more immediately, however, in his catastrophic misjudgment in chapter 5. Ida Wade, too, is not what she appears to Van. He takes pains to avoid scandal by doing what he thinks necessary to prevent the young people of his caste from learning of his dalliance with this "fast girl" he considers farther down the socioeconomic ladder. This is politic. But he makes a mistake in the way he views her personality – a mistake that is understandable in terms of the attitude he developed almost a decade earlier, in chapter 1. Either Van's better self or his brute manifests itself when he determines whether a young woman he is dealing with is a saint or a slut. With Ida, Van decides to feed the brute in a private room at the Imperial Café, where he has sex with this young woman who, unfortunately for him, is neither slut nor saint. The Victorian categories fail; in fact, both characters are victimized by their exercise in this instance.

Normalcy in the Human Animal

As Norris points out, Ida represents a third condition among humanity left out of the formula uncritically applied to her:

> Ida Wade belonged to a certain type of young girl that was very common in the city. She was what men, among each other, called "gay," though that was the worst that could be said of her. She was virtuous, but the very fact that it was necessary to say so was enough to cause the statement to be doubted. . . . She loved to have a "gay" time, which for her meant to drink California champagne, to smoke cigarettes, and to kick at the chandelier. She was still virtuous and meant to stay so; there was nothing vicious about her, and she was as far removed from Flossie's class as from that of Turner Ravis. (*V*, 68-69)

Given that Ida is of a "very common" type for the 1890s, one might hazard a modern description of "normal," just as one might now think of Van as "abnormal," or at least no more sophisticated than Mac in his understanding of human nature. Not interpreting Ida the way Norris has, and classing Ida with Flossie, Van treats her the way one might a prostitute once service has been rendered. The brute satisfied, Van discreetly ignores her.

Why Ida commits suicide is moot, although she is clearly not a calloused whore insensitive to the rejection she experiences. She may also think the way Van does about the better self and the brute within *her*, and guilt thus compounds the ordeal of having been used and discarded by her indifferent "lover." Whatever the precise cause, Van is absolutely dumbfounded that she has reacted so differently than Flossie does after a sexual transaction. Given his saint-versus-slut notions, her suicide is illogical. Van does not come to understand that the formula applied to Ida was inappropriate; indeed, he does not even try to analyze his experience but instead gives himself to guilt and self-pity. Thus, he cannot entertain the possibility that the better-self-versus-brute definition of himself is just as questionable.

The Larger Significance of Van's Vision

As the consequences of Ida's death unfold and Van's step-by-step descent to the condition of a dumb brute progresses, we see that there is more than just Van's simple-minded view of women and his analogous definition of his own dual personality to reconsider. Both perspectives are tied to Van's attitude toward sexual instinct and activity, which in turn is related to his unwavering black-and-white worldview of good and evil. This simplistic moral vision of a 13-year-old seen in a man in his mid-twenties is directly related to the puritanical Christian tradition Van guiltily knows as a Victorian good boy with an ineradicable taste for "vice." This moral vision ultimately relates to the conception of God's view of good and evil derived from the Bible. Victorian moralists, of course, believe in a God with a Victorian viewpoint.

All of this comes into question in *Vandover and the Brute*; for none of it appears validated by events. Indeed, in chapter 9, Van's experience contradicts each of the essential characteristics of the worldview in question. Here, at the center of the novel, Van has the opportunity to examine the morality-related assumptions of his culture to which his mind has conformed. As contradictory evidence shows itself, the possibility that he may free himself from his old mind-set, or mental determinism, is apparent. When this habitual man of leisure does not analyze the data before him, and when the conformist emerges from a revealing new order of experience with the same old ideas, it is clear that he will never achieve independence and a realistic view of things.

Told to do so by his father, Van goes to Coronado Beach near San Diego, at which vacation resort he will stay until the Ida Wade affair becomes a matter of forgotten history. There, amidst social diversions, he adjusts nicely to the unfortunate incident and returns to San Francisco. No change is detectable, for he relies on his old theories for an answer as to how he might better live. He is determined to start anew by being his better self and suppressing the brute. In transit he experiences a shipwreck, and, as the episode recalling Stephen Crane's "The Open Boat" begins, so does Norris's parable for the reader more perceptive than Van. Another kind of subrational prompting than sexual appetite is the issue first offered for consideration, but the generic imagery of irresistible instinct proves familiar, as the deck of Van's ship is "jerked away from beneath his feet": "Vandover's very first impulse was a wild desire of saving himself; he had not the least thought for any one else. Every soul on board might drown, so only he could be saved. It was the primitive animal instinct, the blind adherence to the first great law, and impulse that in this first moment of excitement could not be resisted" (*V*, 128-29).

Van, in short, is not a born altruist. His natural, unmediated response to a threat is to save himself, to don a life preserver – only to find that, as in chapter 1 when moved similarly by the sexual drive, instinct leads him to something shameful. The predictable response of a censorial authority figure in this Victorian microcosm of the ship is to tell Van to desist from the ignoble: "Take this [life preserver] off! there is no danger; you're only exciting the other passengers. Come on, take it off and go back to your berth." The typically docile Van obeys him and observes with chagrin the quite different behavior of a more noble figure than he, a fearless boatswain's mate who goes about calming the passengers. The mate embodies the ideal and is thus a fit subject for representation in *A Home Book of Art*: "He was an inspiration to Vandover, who began to be ashamed of having yielded to the first selfish instinct of preservation" (*V*, 130). Whereupon, the ship begins to capsize.

Following an instinctive prompting has made good sense in this instance. Is it possible, then, that instinct might in some pragmatic way be good and that the "animal" in man might not necessarily be evil? In the instinct-versus-reason conflict, may it be that instinct – of various kinds – is beneficial to the individual? Van has reason to reconsider the whole matter.

The religious tradition that nurtured the worldview in which the instinctive dimension of man was long maligned next receives attention. A fundamentalist Christian, a Salvation Army lassie, is as confident as the steward and the mate were:

> "I'm going to be saved. . . . Jesus is going to save me. I *know* I'm going to be saved. I feel it, I feel it *here*," and she struck her palm on the breast of the man's red jersey she was wearing.
>
> "Well, I wish *I* could have such a confidence," answered Vandover, sincerely envying the plain little woman under the ugly blue bonnet.
>
> She seemed as if inspired, her face glowing. "Only *believe*; that's all," she told him. (*V*, 133)

As Van will soon have the opportunity to discover, when silence is the answer to his prayer for help from God following his father's death (*V*, 243-45), such metaphysically derived "certainties" are dubious. This one is not verified. The "boom of the foremast . . . swung across the deck. . . . Vandover was already out of its path but it struck the young woman squarely across the back. She dropped in a heap . . . her eyes rapidly opened and shut, and a great puff of white froth slowly started from her mouth" (*V*, 136). Like Herman Melville with *Moby-Dick*, Norris here entitled himself to the claim that he had written a wicked, perhaps blasphemous book; here the allusion is to the promise of divine aid frequently articulated in the Bible and given its best-known phrasing in Psalm 23. If the biblical definition of the deity and the interpretation of God's will which is the origin of Van's concepts of good versus evil are askew, Van has reason to reconsider all of the a prioris that have shaped his life. So too do Norris's 1890s readers.

The contradictions continue. Chapter 1 again comes to mind, when Van the artist is not experiencing a shipwreck secondhand in the likes of *A Home Book of Art* but enduring the real thing: "There was nothing picturesque about it all, nothing heroic. It was unlike any pictures he had seen of lifeboat rescues, unlike anything he had ever imagined. It was all sordid, miserable, and the sight of the half-clad women, dirty, sodden, unkempt, stirred him rather to disgust than to pity" (*V*, 143). Here we have the requisite vignette for a novelist associated with the Realism and Naturalism movements and their animus toward Romantic idealism. The ideal image – the way things *should* be as represented in conventional art – is placed in ironic juxtaposition with the real, and here one would expect Van, who knows more about art than anything else, to begin discerning that he has been betrayed by art as well as Victorian ethics. But he does not. Unlike the reader, Van learns nothing about the potential and actual value of instinct, the relationship between a better side of his nature and the animalistic side, the inadequacies of the religious "certainties" that informed his thought, or the relationship between life and art.[6]

He may have developed one insight, though. Back in San Francisco, a waiter at the Imperial Café accosts him with the report that the first engineer of the ship is in trouble with the civil authorities. He has had to kill Brann, a diamond salesman who threatened to capsize Van's overfilled lifeboat. The lives of all in the boat were at stake, and Brann's life had to be sacrificed. Van appears to know that the waiter is wrong when declaring, "A thing like that is regular murder." It was not. Murder at a cotillion is one thing and not at all what occurred at sea: different circumstances shed different light on legal and moral principles. Ever-conventional Van, however, does not respond; rather, "Vandover shut his teeth against answering" and, "with delicious enjoyment," treats himself to "oysters, an omelette, and a pint of claret" (*V*, 150). Again, nothing has changed. It appears that Van can adjust to any situation as long as he is not obliged to abandon his childlike perception of right and wrong, good and evil, saints and sinners.

The Downward Movement

In chapter 10, the long slide begins with his father's death and Van's inept managing of his own affairs. In chapter 13, he riotously returns to vice with "a debauch of forty-eight hours" (*V*, 209); in chapter 14, a performance of Charles Gounod's opera *Faust* inspires him once again to suppress the brute and to devote himself to the only good thing left to him from the wreckage of his life: his art.[7] The renewed vacillation between the two extremes, however, soon ends. Van's life changes, but not as he hoped. By the close of chapter 14, he discovers that he cannot execute a drawing he has begun; gone, it seems, is the talent that always showed "the strongest side of him" and is "the one thing that could save him" (*V*, 220). Alone, Van looks out his studio window and reflects on the noises rising from the city. The narrative voice has modulated to free indirect discourse:

> It was Life, the murmur of the great, mysterious force that spun the wheels of Nature and that sent it onward like some enormous engine, resistless, relentless; an engine that sped straight forward, driving before it the infinite herd of humanity, driving it on at breathless speed through all eternity, driving it no one knew whither, crushing inexorably all those who lagged behind the herd and who fell from exhaustion, grinding them to dust beneath its myriad iron wheels, riding over them, still driving on the herd that yet remained, driving it recklessly, blindly on and on toward some far-distant goal, some vague unknown end, some mysterious, fearful bourne forever hidden in the thick darkness. (*V*, 230-31)

As Norris approximates Van's impression of some "infinitely great monster" that the urban scene before him suggests, what is most noteworthy about the perspective is that Van now sees himself as absolutely powerless, as one of the "herd" *driven* toward some mysterious goal. His view of his life is radically deterministic; he sees no way to escape being one of the herd.

When the experience and the same imagery of the "vast fearful engine" recur in chapter 15, Van goes beyond blaming life in general for his condition. Or, rather, he returns to his old, moralistic point of view. The guilt-ridden Victorian once more proves that he learned nothing during the shipwreck experience. He believes that he is now being punished, personally, for his sinful life: "It was the punishment that he had brought upon himself, . . . the result of his long indulgence of vice, his vile submission to the brute that was to destroy his reason" (*V*, 243). He blames the brute-within that is now eliminating the instinct-versus-reason conflict by debilitating his mind. As the syphilis does just that, Van adjusts to what he sees as the wages of sin. Playing the brute in earnest, he gives in wholly to vice and spends all of his estate. His wild alcoholism accelerates his decline into dementia, made all the more sensational by his conviction that he is literally a wolf: we see him one evening taking off his clothes and "yielding in a second to the strange hallucination of that four-footed thing that sulked and snarled. . . . Naked, four-footed, Vandover ran back and forth the length of the room" (*V*, 310). Generally, though, he dully drifts into the numbed condition in which he is last seen, removing the offal from one of Charlie Geary's cottages. The healthy young brute tracing a scent in chapter 1 is a sick creature slated for extinction.

The Nature of Instinct

Vandover and the Brute is the third (and penultimate) novel in which Norris makes the concept of instinct central. *A Man's Woman, The Octopus,* and *The Pit* do not ignore this concept, but it does not receive the attention Norris granted it in his first four novels. It would seem, in short, that he had his say by the time that the publication of *Blix* followed that of *McTeague,* in the fall of 1899. Like "every child of man," as Norris phrased it in *McTeague,* Van was

called on to face the fact of sexual appetite and consider what un-
prejudiced rational response to it, and all instincts, is appropriate.
When the adults in the lifeboat sanction the sacrifice of Brann as
they respond to the "animal in them . . . the primal instinct of the
brute striving for its life and the life of its young" (V,140), they all
participate in the killing, and we are not sure whether that instinctive
response is "right" or "wrong," or even if there is an available moral
category that applies. Forty survived because they did not observe
the absolute of "Thou shalt not kill."

Norris does not replace an old absolute with a new one, however. He instead pushes the reader to do what Van did not: to think
and choose situationally, without a priori interpretations distorting
one's decisions. Chapter 9 crystallizes this issue through the
questions it raises: *Which* instincts should be followed? *How* should
they be translated into action? *What* modifications in Western
attitudes toward the irrational in man should be effected once it is
realized that natural drives are not in themselves "evil"?[8] *How*
appropriate to life as it actually is are the biblical concepts which
Victorians chose to emphasize? Chapters 10 through 18 illustrate
what may occur if such questions are not posed.

Chapter Five

Blix and *A Man's Woman*

Foray into Eden

Blix stands out in the Norris canon as the least complicated and most positive novel. It is also his most autobiographical. Condy Rivers writes for a San Francisco newspaper as Norris did for *The Wave* in 1896-98. He finally becomes serious about his work, transcending his dilatoriness as a journalist as well as his stalled career as a fictionalist. Acting on the recommendation of an Eastern publisher who has declined a collection of his stories, he produces a novel of action and adventure distinctly like *Moran of the Lady Letty*. Its title is Norris's gloss on the ungenteel, anti-Victorian character of *Moran*: Condy names it *In Defiance of Authority*. Like Norris, he is offered a position with the publisher in New York. As the novel closes, he feels that he finally has his life in order and is ready to meet the challenges that lie ahead. *Blix* is not an ambiguous book like *Moran* or an ambivalent one like *McTeague*. It is a tale as joyous as *Vandover* is pathetic.

While sketches related to it were produced at Harvard in 1894-95, the plot was not accessible until 1896-1898 when Norris's experiences given to Condy occurred. Furthermore, it was not until 1897-98 that his relationship with Jeannette Black became similar to the one Condy enjoys with Travis Bessemer, or "Blix." It is likely, then, that Norris developed some of the manuscript after he received the call from New York on 14 February 1898; he most likely worked on it more between August and October when recuperating in San Francisco from the malaria contracted in Cuba, finishing it that fall and winter in New York. It was serialized in *The Puritan* beginning in March 1899 and, after a thorough revision of its beginning, was published by Doubleday & McClure Co. in September.

Norris's problems when returning to San Francisco in August 1898 were not only physical. Having seen in Cuba the grisly evidence of a young girl raped and murdered, wide-scale hunger, and other far from romantic aspects of wartime, he made his depression clear in a letter to Ernest Peixotto before he left New York (*Letters*, 52-53). The time spent with his family and friends helped him get over that. That spent with Jeannette, however, must have been even more invigorating. While *Blix* was dedicated to his mother, the portrait of the heroine is an unqualified celebration of Jeannette. For the first time since *Yvernelle*, Norris had something in common with Victorian idealists: "ideal womanhood," a concept that was undermined variously in the first three novels, had again become meaningful to him.[1] The vibrant young Californienne depicted is as noble as any woman is ever likely to become – in Norris's eyes at least.

The "California Girl" Theme

This is the first way that Norris dotes on Travis, in the context of popular interest regarding how the buxom "California Girl" differed from her comparatively frail and anemic sisters in the East. Travis embodies the "beautiful girl" of the type: "She was young, but tall as most men, and solidly, almost heavily built. Her shoulders were broad, her chest was deep, her neck round and firm. She radiated health; there were exuberance and vitality in the very touch of her foot upon the carpet, and there was that cleanness about her, that freshness, that suggested a recent plunge in the surf and a 'constitutional' along the beach. One felt that here was stamina, good physical force, and fine animal vigor."[2] That the last sentence might bring to mind an evaluation of a thoroughbred racehorse or a mare being considered for breeding purposes spells the difference between Norris's idealization and those of Victorians. Dickens hardly pictured Agnes thus in *David Copperfield* or Coventry Patmore his Honoria in *The Angel in the House*, but Norris proved consistent in regard to his previous loyalty to the concept of the human animal, this time giving it a wholly positive emphasis the way that James Lane Allen did in 1896 in *A Summer in Arcady*. Travis has the beauty and virtue of an Agnes, *plus* the less than angelic qualities of a normal, postpubescent female. Her "fine animal vigor" does not preclude virtue, sensitivity, and an uncommon intelligence. Travis is a superior example of the breed, and her sexuality – while not strongly emphasized in *Blix* – is apparent. Norris's long paean to the hearty California beauty ends with a then-erotic image: "with every movement there emanated from her a barely perceptible delicious feminine odor – an odor that was in part perfume, but mostly a subtle, vague smell, charming beyond words, that came from her hair, her neck, her arms – her whole sweet personality. She was nineteen years old" (*B*, 9).

The "New Woman"

That Travis is a "good, sweet, natural, healthy-minded, healthy-bodied girl, honest, strong, self-reliant, and good-tempered" (*B*, 8) is seen repeatedly in the novel, but the beginning of the main plot results from the especially bold display of one of these traits: self-reliance. When her beau, Condy, arrives at her home, she announces that she is tired of conforming to upper middle-class expectations for young ladies: "I'm done with conventionality for good. I am going to try . . . to be just as true to myself as I can be. . . . I'm going to do the things that I like to do – just so long as they are the things a good girl can do" (*B*, 37). And so she begins. She wants to drop all hypocrisies, such as the self-serving pretence that she loves Condy. She forces Condy – also fatigued with the artifice of being informally engaged – to admit that he does not love her either. Matching her honesty, he is relieved to find that he too is free from a relationship that is flat. True to his own penchant for the unconventional, Norris has begun a love story by inverting the typical structure: this one begins with Travis's and Condy's declarations that they are *not* in love and their vow that they will not even mention the word thenceforth. "No more foolishness" is their motto, frankness their byword.

By the close of chapter 2, then, Travis has a second culturally significant identity as well: acting so pluckily before a male who, as friend rather than dissembling "lover," is her equal, she initiates a "revolution" (*B*, 40). Henceforth, she types the "New Woman" figure also receiving attention in 1890s periodicals. Like Henry James's Daisy Miller she goes where she chooses, does what she likes, and says what she thinks; unlike Daisy's would-be lover, Winterbourne, Condy respects the self-directed character she displays. When she meets Condy in the street the next day, she chooses to accompany him to the waterfront where he is to report on a steamer taking on grain for famine-stricken India. This is better than cotillions; even better is hearing a fanciful yarn spun by a mate, which Condy can use for a short story. Travis shows a previously unseen side of her personality as she proves as enthusiastic about the fictional possibilities as he: "Condy was astonished and delighted to note that she 'caught on' to the idea as quickly as he, and knew the telling points and what details to leave out" (B, 60).

Later, as the two lunch at a restaurant in Chinatown, Condy reads to her from his beloved Kipling. She again reveals her acuity when she praises Kipling for an effect that Condy admires highly. It is clear what the bases for their active friendship will be: for the first time, they display without reserve their naturally lively and light-hearted personalities, and they like what they see in each other now that the masks have been removed. They soon find that they enjoy together the quasi-bohemian activities available to journalists searching for articles. As they ramble about and explore the San Francisco landscape, Travis's curiosity about the mechanics of literary creation proves another experiential bond that becomes stronger as she takes an increasing interest in his career. She helps him in writing the mate's tale as "A Victory over Death."

If friendship is of the essence in an ideal male-female relationship – as appears Norris's theme – one wonders how long it will take before the pledge to refrain from lovemaking is broken. What could be more natural and promising than increasingly enhanced friendship transmuting into what may be termed "love," even "ideal love"? Readers whose curiosity is engaged will proceed, wondering *how* the transition will occur. Those who find the drift a bit too obvious will halt. The student of Norris, however, has an extra incentive to continue: When love flowers, will Norris provide a positive description of human sexuality, free from the stresses of Victorian morality seen in *McTeague* and *Vandover*? Will Condy find his arousal as complex an experience as McTeague and Vandover did? How will Travis compare with Trina Sieppe and Ida Wade? Finally, will two individuals whose love grew out of shared interests and activities fare better than those, like Norris's parents, whose relationship did not include the same?

The Maturation Problem

The answers to these questions are forestalled as Norris describes the activities of the hero and heroine via a panoramic piece of local-color fiction featuring Condy's and Travis's high-jinking adventures in and about the city. They enjoy the vista of the Golden Gate as they stroll beyond the Presidio, picnic and fish together at Lake San Andreas, engage in matchmaking between an old salt, Captain Jack, and a woman named K.D.B., read more Kipling, and generally behave like carefree children on a holiday. The New Woman figure, however, will not continue thus, to someday be taken care of by a charming male breadwinner. Travis is already making plans for a different kind of future: she is hoping to go to New York to study medicine. Condy protests, revealing that he is not quite so liberated from gender biases as his friend: "It isn't as though you had to support yourself." Travis's response immediately separates her from the generation of Gertrude Norris: "One must have some occupation; and isn't studying medicine, Condy, better than piano-playing, or French courses, or literary classes and Browning circles? Oh, I've no patience with that kind of girl!" (*B*, 199). Condy sees her point of view, taking a long step away from conventional attitudes. Indeed, he displays a remarkable disinterest in her welfare: "I like the idea of *you* studying something. It would be the making of such a girl as you, Blix" (*B*, 199-200). The unpleasant notion of thus losing his chum does not result in his attempting to prevent her from discomfiting him. He is as interested in her making something of her life as she is in his success.

It seems relevant to note here that Norris's mother did not care for Travis's real-life counterpart, the free-spirited Jeannette Black who also dropped out of high society. The novel is as much a defense of Norris's fiancée before his mother as it is a celebration. Furthermore, Travis's derogatory reference to participation in Browning circles of the type Gertrude headed is interpretable as Norris's well-aimed dart in *Blix* – anticipating the fuller criticism to appear in *The Pit*, where that other "kind of girl" is the unstable, Gertrude-like heroine.

Travis is true to her word. As *Blix* ends, she is preparing to depart for her studies in the East. Maturation is, in short, a relatively easy process through which the liberated young woman is passing as she sets clear goals and achieves them. On the other hand, Condy's life is considerably more complicated because it reflects Norris's own experience during the *Wave* years and the long-standing complexities related to his uneasy relationship to his mother, as just seen

in the gibe at her. That Condy is living with his mother is only mentioned once, and so *Blix* does not directly examine her influence on
him. Shown only is his profound immaturity, a kind of
"youthfulness" that is not unattractive in 19-year-old Travis. But it is
inappropriate in the much older Condy. At 28, he goofily recites lim-
ericks the afternoon that Travis and he have lunch in Chinatown. He
also plays the banjo for her there, cutting up with an exaggerated
rendition of a ragtime "coon-song." He is, in short, playing the
fool – suddenly realizing that he appears a superannuated fraternity
boy and self-consciously apologizing for that. Travis, on the other
hand, is delighted, for she is the age of a sorority sister and is not
viewing Condy from the vantage point of 28. But the reader, and
Norris, have a different perspective. Condy *is* acting as though he is
only 19 or younger, just as he is a irresponsible journalist who cannot meet deadlines and a fictionalist who cannot make the grade. In
addition, he is addicted to gambling. Norris's self-portrait is not a
flattering one.

Travis as Enabler

Jeannette Black qua Travis Bessemer is in effect the deus ex machina
in the Norris qua Condy tale, receiving full credit for accomplishing
what two incompetent parents and upper-middle-class institutions
did not. The fictional testimony to Travis emphasizes, first, that she
accepts Condy as he is, having faith in his positive characteristics as
she notes his shortcomings without carping. Second, she is totally
supportive with regard to the obvious means of elevating his self-es-
teem and increasing his seriousness: as with herself vis-à-vis an
"occupation," she sees Condy's desired career as a fictionalist as the
way to give shape to his dilettantish life. Third, she also cares enough
to lend a hand with the gambling problem that consumes his time
and money. She initiates a scheme that, as it turns out, positions
Condy for his escape from his old ways: Condy will come to her
when the urge to gamble is on him, and they will play poker. Preter-
naturally unlucky at cards, Condy loses each time, and Travis privately saves her winnings. It finally amounts to a month's wages for
Condy. The time spent together pays another dividend as well:
Condy is weaned from gambling as he discovers other activities that
are more pleasurable, also according to Travis's plan.

The positive consequence is twofold. Aided by the old salt, Captain Jack, as well as his shoptalking chum, Condy has developed an outline for his short novel of action and adventure, but he cannot execute it because his newspaper will not allow him the time necessary. Travis brings forth her winnings, returning Condy's money so that he may drop his "hack work" (*B*, 280) and devote all of his time to the novel. Initially chagrined, he accepts her plan. Ironically, the novel is rejected, but, in drawing attention to himself thus, he has captured the attention of the publisher to whom he sent it. The Centennial Publishing Company in New York has noticed his previously published short story, "A Victory over Death," and offers him a position. Free from gambling, having learned self-discipline and responsibility by completing the novel as he promised Travis, and having earned a berth with a major publisher, Condy is finally moving forward – thanks to Travis.

The second result of gambling with Travis instead of his clubmen acquaintances is that Condy has spent more time with her, developing a new and healthy "addiction." He is intensely in love with Travis.

The Brute in Blix

As a love-idyll, *künstlerroman*, and criticism of the social values of 1890s America, *Blix* does not disappoint. While the plot is predictable in its episodic accretion of experiences leading to the full flowering of love – on New Year's Eve no less – the joie de vivre displayed and the attraction of reading a happy tale so unique to the Norris canon compensate for a translucence that might otherwise irritate. What does disappoint, though, is Norris's decision not to treat the "sex problem" – or, rather, his not showing how sex may not necessarily be a problem for so mature a heroine and a hero rapidly moving beyond his boyishness.

Norris does whet our appetite for a positive handling of sex the day Condy first realizes that he loves Travis. As they stroll along the Pacific coast on a "royal morning," Condy and Blix are found in their happiest state so far in the novel – a state in which reason sleeps in the human animal:

> The simple things of the world, the great, broad, primal emotions of the race
> stirred in them. As they swung along, going toward the ocean, their brains

were almost as empty of thought or of reflection as those of two fine, clean animals. They were all for the immediate sensation; they did not think – they *felt*. The intellect was dormant; they looked at things, they heard things, they smelt the smell of the sea, and of the seaweed, of the fat, rank growth of cresses in the salt marshes; they turned their cheeks to the passing wind, and filled their mouths and breasts with it. (*B*, 237-38)

It is then that Condy realizes his freedom from worry and feelings of inadequacy, as well as the unprecedented joy he is experiencing. Turning to the woman at his side, he sees the cause for the happy effect, and he loves her. What the reader sees in addition is that the "primal emotions of the race" are stirring these "fine, clean animals" and that they are thus positioned for spontaneous, natural responses of the kind that may occur when the intellect becomes "dormant" and sensory perceptions are heightened.

The opportunity to synthesize Victorian idealism with a Naturalistic concept of the human sexuality then follows as Condy reflects on the ideality of Travis: her "goodness" and "clean purity and womanliness." Condy reacts with high Victorian morality, as "he felt his nobler side rousing up and the awakening of the desire to be his better self" (*B*, 249-50). Immediately before this, however, he had a different sort of experience as he focused on her physicality. Travis's scent is again described, as another kind of arousal occurs: "There emanated from her with every movement a barely perceptible, delicious, feminine odor" (*B*, 249). Both erotic and what may be termed Platonic imagery inform the scene, and – significantly – no trauma is recorded. The "better self" is *not* in conflict with "the brute" as in *McTeague* and *Vandover*.

Yet once more, Norris brings himself to the verge of a positive, post-Victorian treatment of sexuality when the earlier impediment to lovemaking – the vow not to talk of love taken by Condy and Travis – has been removed. The two return to the same scene on the coast after they declare their love, and, once again, the intellect gives way to "the broad, simpler, basic emotions, the fundamental instincts of the race" (*B*, 327). Nature gives them "a sensation as of a bigness and a return to the homely, human, natural life, to the primitive old impulses, irresistible, changeless, and unhampered" (*B*, 328). This is the moment for the emergence of the brute in both, as the intellect is "drowsy and numb" and "the emotions, the senses, [are] all alive and brimming to the surface."

Travis announces that she now feels she has become "a woman": "A little trembling ran through her with the words. She stopped and put both arms around his neck, her head tipped back, her eyes half closed, her sweet yellow hair rolling from her forehead. Her whole dear being radiated with that sweet, clean perfume that seemed to come alike from her clothes, her neck, her arms, her hair, and mouth – the delicious, almost divine, feminine aroma that was part of herself" (*B*, 330). Whereupon, with the erotic semantically linked to the "divine" and the possibility that these nice young people will not appear ignoble as they exercise their sexuality, Norris defaults. This is as far as he takes his characters. Despite the evocative imagery and the opportunity to show how human sexuality may be a positive expression of genuine love, Norris chose to emphasize the idea that "pure, unselfish affection, young and unstained," developed "almost without thought of sex" (*B*, 326). Had Norris proceeded with the logic of a truly Naturalistic portrayal of his characters, *Blix* might have been as precedent-setting a cultural document as *McTeague*.

An End to Eden

Rather than restart the work with the theme of sexual initiation, Norris moved to closure with another, less specific and all-embracing rite of passage experience. He focused on adulthood per se, executing a Bouguereau-like allegorical representation of Youth on the verge of leaving its comparatively Edenic realm of simplicity. Appropriately, the elegiac note is sounded, and, quite consistently for the allusive author of *McTeague* and *Vandover*, the myth of man's fall in Genesis is the means of commemorating the loss of childlike innocence – although it is a guilt-free "fall" that is recorded as both characters prepare to leave home for New York. *Blix* ends mythically with Condy and Blix elevated to the status of archetypes leaving a Garden and entering the world that adults know, where one earns his living by the sweat of his and – with the New Woman on the scene – *her* brow: "Their little gayeties were done; the life of little things was all behind. Now for the future. The sterner note had struck – work to be done; that, too, the New Year had brought to them – work for each of them, work and the world of men. For a moment they shrank from it, loath to take the first step beyond the confines of the garden wherein they had lived so joyously and learned to love each other" (*B*, 338). As they move forward, neither character is burdened with "the knowledge of good and evil" that was part and parcel of Van's and Mac's traumatic "fall" into adulthood.[3] Moreover, that Condy and Blix choose to leave the Garden spells another telling difference: *they* have decided that they are ready to take next step in the maturation process and are psychologically prepared to deal with the complexities to be encountered.

Life outside the Garden

A Man's Woman might have been a curiosity-satisfying sequel in which Norris demonstrated how conjugal love is dealt with by a Condy and a Travis at the close of the nineteenth century. This novel, however, did not develop that way. It was possibly begun between August and October 1898, when Norris was in San Francisco; by February or March 1899, Norris was expeditiously developing two subjects and character types he had focused on during the *Wave* years, confidently viewing them as the surefire means to a riveting novel. As *The Wave* had repeatedly indicated, the quest to reach the North Pole was full of marketplace potential, and Norris had already capitalized on this topic in 1897 with "The End of the Beginning."[4] This became the first draft of chapters 1 and 2, wherein explorer Ward Bennett's sufferings during an Arctic expedition are recorded with a specificity made possible by Norris's reading on the subject. Jeannette Norris told Franklin Walker that her husband was also coached by Captain Joseph Hodgson – Captain Jack in *Blix* – whom the Norrises had met in 1897. "Love interest" being an essential for popular appeal, Norris again brought forward a representative of the New Woman. The *Wave* piece to which this figure was related is "The Evolution of a Nurse,"[5] which describes the training of and demands on nurses – details that accelerated Norris's development of Lloyd Searight's characterization in chapter 3. More information and the medical language Norris would require for verisimilitude came from his fraternity brother, Dr. Albert Houston, to whom he dedicated the book.

Inversion: Love without Friendship

Sex aside because it does not figure at all in *A Man's Woman*, the novel is similar to *Blix* in its focus on the male-female relationship. This time, though, Norris chose to treat the topic in problematic rather than paradigmatic terms; simply stated, *everything* goes wrong in the Ward-Lloyd relationship. Indeed, just as *Blix* directly relates to Norris's happy relationship with Jeannette, *A Man's Woman* appears a brooding anticipation of the fictional reworking of the B.F.-Gertrude debacle in *The Pit*. It is the story of two colossal egotists, like Norris's parents, who become combatants as they attempt to use each other to meet their own needs.

The first two chapters portray the titanic willpower of Ward, who, failing to reach the North Pole, maniacally drives his men and himself southward where they may be rescued by a whaler. Those who cannot keep up are remorselessly left behind by Ward, and "the fittest" are saved owing to his unwavering resolve – just after chief engineer Richard Ferriss comforts the apparently doomed Ward with the fib that Lloyd Searight secretly loves him. Having won at least one battle against Nature, the doughty survivor returns home savoring a more gratifying conquest: he believes that his ideal woman is already his. He is one of those uncomplicated "men of single ideas" who approaches all tasks with as much fixed determination as he displayed in the Arctic.[6] Claiming the woman who loves him is his first concern. He little realizes that Lloyd is as formidable the Arctic – and a good deal more complicated.

Chapter 3 reveals that Ward's dream maiden bears minimal resemblance to Travis. A wealthy orphan who has countered as best she can her personal insecurities by creating a larger-than-life personality, she is the female counterpart of Ward: a no-nonsense achiever, a self-made professional relentlessly dedicated to the goals of being the perfect nurse and escaping the vulnerabilities of mere, weak women. Psychologically, she is as grotesque as the androgynous heroine of *Moran*. In one moment of free indirect discourse, Norris discloses the self-conscious rebellion from conventional female roles that is hers now that she runs her own nursing agency: "Ah! she was better than other women; ah! she was stronger than other women; she was carrying out a splendid work. She straightened herself to her full height abruptly, stretching her outspread hands vaguely to the sunlight, to the City, to the world, to the great engine of life whose lever she could grasp and could control, smiling proudly, almost insolently, in the consciousness of her strength, the fine steadfastness of her purpose" (*W*, 57-58). He also reveals in the same scene that, unlike Travis, she is quite neurotic. The megalomaniacal vision of controlling the great engine of life offers relief during an anxiety attack: dread overwhelms her when she thinks about the fate of the Arctic expedition and, as we find in chapter 4, Ward Bennett. One suspects that there is more of the mere, weak woman in her than she can accept.

As Lloyd makes clear in a monologue beginning "Oh, if I were a man!" (*W*, 81), she has turned to nursing as an available gender-based substitute for exploring and like endeavors not then possible for women. Ward will someday conquer the frozen North; Lloyd, who has recognized Ward as her role model, will conquer disease. It is no wonder Ward has praised her as "a man's woman" (*W*, 40), and no wonder that she is this egotist's ideal. He admires in her the very traits that are his own; his love is a form of self-love. She, as is clear in chapter 4, is infatuated with those traits in Ward she has labored to make *her* own. It would seem that a perfect match between identical types is in the offing – but for three problems.

The first is that they know each as heroic, but only in imagination. They are acquaintances at most, rather than friends, and they appear to have remained each other's dream figure because they are *not* familiar with each other's personality quirks. Second, while Richard sees their congruity – "What a pair they were, strong, masterful both, insolent in the consciousness of their power!" (*W*, 40) – he does not reflect on what is predictable when two such Nietzschean superpersons occupy the same space and the struggle for dominance commences. Lloyd Searight will hardly play the cow before this bull. Third, although Ward hails from the civilized world, he is even more unsocialized than the prickly, introverted Lloyd; courtship requires finesse, especially with a woman with as exalted a view of herself as Lloyd has, and Ward errs when approaching her like a mail-order bride delivered for him at the local train depot. His entire courtship of the woman he barely seems to know takes less than five minutes, and even then he is exasperated to have taken so long to come to the point after the long hike to her country home, during which he has been examining rock samples: " 'Miss Searight,' he began, his harsh, bass voice pitched even lower than usual, 'what do you think I am down here for? This is not the only part of the world where I could recuperate, I suppose, and as for spending God's day in chipping at stones, like a professor of a young ladies' seminary' – he hurled the hammer from him into the bushes – 'that for geology! Now we can talk. You know very well that I love you, and I believe that you love me. I have come down here to ask you to marry me' " (*W*, 137). Love, as defined in *Blix*, is not what we find here as Ward reveals his utter ignorance of Lloyd's personality. The "you" addressed is a blank on the map.

Lloyd is astounded by such treatment because there is no way Ward can know that she does secretly love him. She is also crest-fallen: it was a boost to her ego when she found that this extraordinary man wanted to see her extraordinary self before all others on his return, and she had hoped for further testimony to her regal worth, her success in making herself his equal. In addition, the titaness who has governed the great engine of life is suddenly a vulnerable figure – like "other women" – now that her secret is out. Denial is her only defense.

When Lloyd reacts with hauteur, Ward makes the worst mistake imaginable. He accuses her of one of the traits of the mere-woman figure she loathes: he chides her for acting the coquette. He is beyond such conventional behavior. She should be too: "Good God! are you not big enough to be above such things?" (*W*, 108). She, of course, prefers to think of herself as that big, and then some. She denounces the tale Richard told, but Ward cannot believe that a comrade who is more than a brother would lie. The unpleasant scene ends with Ward dispatched, *but unrelenting in his love*. Lloyd *still loves him*, we quickly learn, but Richard's tale has "put her in a position . . . galling to her pride, her dignity"; how could Ward believe "that she had so demeaned herself " (*W*, 110-11) by confessing her love to Richard as a giddy girl might? Ward is outraged with Lloyd; Lloyd is enraged. *And yet they remain in love*. It would seem that both are incapable of recognizing that a mistake has been made. Each having decided that the other is lovable, neither can countenance the idea of being in error.

Round Two

The wilful lovers separated, they are quickly brought back together in the grand scene that is chapter 6. When Ward learns that the bat-

tler against disease is undaunted when called on to nurse a
contagious typhoid victim, he rushes to her to prevent her from doing what he would heroically do in his respective sphere. Love is his
justification; control is his habit. Not to do her duty is for Lloyd to
surrender her self-conception as well as her unblemished reputation
with her colleagues. And so the high melodrama develops in a passage that is positively operatic. Ward staggers before Lloyd as she
parries and then thrusts: the typhoid patient in the next room is no
other than Richard Ferriss. Ward must chose between the woman he
loves and his best friend. He blocks the sickroom door, saving Lloyd
as he loses his friend to typhoid. He also loses Lloyd who has, in effect, lost everything because of her failure to embody the perfect
nurse.

Chapter 7 is given to Lloyd's morose ruminations as she faces the
ruin of her carefully crafted life. She passes from hatred of Ward to
studied indifference. She then returns to work, determined to live
down her past. Chapter 8 is devoted to Ward's introspections. Apparently never having experienced self-doubt or even considered the
possibility that he might be fallible, he now wonders if he made the
right decision. "Hitherto Bennett's only salvation from absolute de-
spair had been the firm consciousness of his own rectitude" (*W*,
195). Now he finds that uncertainty keeps insinuating itself: "Then it
became terrible. Alone there, in the darkness and in the night, Bennett went down into the pit" (*W*, 197). The doubt becomes a
certainty of his inadequacies and, now on a level with imperfect
Lloyd, he faces *his* failure.

The Humanization of the Titans

Introduced as equals in the framework of the heroic saga, Ward and
Lloyd are ground down to more human proportions by experience.
They finally begin to have something in common beyond their fantasies of the way things should be: failure. Their former roles as
perfectionists demanding that life fit the scenarios they have devised
are gradually sloughed as misery produces a new kind of equality. It
only remains for Norris to reunite them in the right circumstances in
order to have them begin demonstrating a commonplace consequence of the experience of suffering: sensitivity to the condition of
others.

Abandoning his career as explorer, disheartened and guilt-ridden Ward is determined to make amends for his past by writing his expedition's memoir with Richard the hero of the tale. This, however, will not bring Lloyd and him together, and the plot develops accordingly: typhoid again rears its ugly head. Struck down, Ward occupies the bed in which Richard suffered, where he may be relieved of more guilt as he passes through the same affliction. Lloyd hears of the new typhoid case and leaps at the opportunity to clear her reputation as well as *her* guilty conscience. It is the same house and the same sickroom, but the principals have changed since they last clashed wills. Lloyd finds a helpless man, absolutely dependent on her ministrations – a man whose obsession with Richard is revealed in his rantings. She realizes how much he loved her when sacrificing his comrade. Furthermore, when Ward briefly regains consciousness, he thinks of Lloyd before himself, attempting to make her leave the sickroom. The depth of his love is clear: he is willing to sacrifice his own life for her welfare. In short, she comes to *understand*, and love is reenthroned in her breast. Chapter 8 ends with the problem solved. When Ward regains full consciousness, he tells her that he does *not* want her to leave the sickroom now. She will not leave him: "Never, never, dearest; never so long as I shall live" (*W*, 227).

It was not Norris's finest moment, and he knew it. In a 22 November 1899 letter to journalist Isaac F. Marcosson, he derided *A Man's Woman* as a "niggling analysis" (*Letters*, 92-93).

A Blixean Reprise

According to his widow, Norris was seriously ill during the winter of 1898-99, and it appears that he did not finish the novel for its serialization in the *San Francisco Chronicle* beginning in September until the late spring or summer of 1899 when he was researching *The Octopus* in California. The remainder of *A Man's Woman* strongly suggests that there was an interval in the composition between the sickroom scene and what follows. In chapter 9, Ward has recuperated and is keeping house with Lloyd and his factotum, Adler. Unfortunately, Ward is not the same character the reader knows. That Norris at some point decided to bring his characters closer to Condy's and Travis's condition is suddenly obvious. For, *tout à coup*, these well-read, outgoing, playful spirits of the previous novel

have returned with new names. The near-Neanderthal Ward is now a
jolly chap, good-naturedly grousing about his milk diet and guying
Lloyd when she relates that she must return to her work. He pre-
tends a relapse at that moment. Who would have thought that he was
such a wag?

The frenetically driven nurse, too, now has a scintillating
personality. Both even prove ready to engage in literary high jinks
when Lloyd receives a letter from the father of a former patient: it is a
marriage proposal. The occasion invites effervescent drollery from
the two wits with their tongues in their cheeks:

> "To mum – mar – marry him? Well, damn his impudence!"
>
> "Mr. Campbell is an eminently respectable and worthy gentleman."
>
> "Oh, well, I don't care. Go! Go, marry Mr. Campbell. Be happy! I forgive
> you both. Go, leave me to die alone."
>
> "Sir, I will go. Forget that you ever knew an unhappy wom – female,
> whose only fault was that she loved you."
>
> "Go! and sometimes think of me far away on the billow and drop a silent
> tear – I say, how are you going to answer Campbell's letter?" (W, 234)

Ward's "I say," delivered with the aplomb of a stage-door johnny, is
particularly egregious. If one has accepted the "reality" of this novel
thus far, the deconstruction is total in this violation of the image already in place. Suffering may produce sensitivity and reveal affinities,
but it does not normally render one a fraternity house swell ready to
trade bons mots with a cotillion queen. The Blixean infusion does,
however, facilitate the movement toward the inevitable: delighting in
each other thus, they plan for their marriage. Conceptually, love finally makes sense now that the hero and heroine have spent some
time getting to know each other, but Norris had to create new
personalities for his characters to accomplish the resolution.

The "New Woman" Revisited

Another peculiarity surfaces as the novel ends. The ideal woman
typed by Travis is, in part, replicated in Lloyd. Having moved beyond
self-centeredness, Lloyd is sensitive to the fact that Ward – a man of
action – cannot possibly find fulfillment as a chronicler of his expedition. What *is* he going to do with the rest of his life? This is answered quickly, via the previously positioned deus ex machina of
Lloyd's personal wealth. Lloyd does what Blix did: she makes it pos-

sible for Ward to pursue his career by restimulating his interest in the
Polar quest, finding public funding for the enterprise and making up
the shortfall herself. When Travis did the same for Condy, he
proclaimed her a "man's woman": "If you loved a man, you'd be a
regular pal to him; you'd back him up, you'd stand by him till the last
gun was fired"*(B,* 279). Lloyd has earned the sobriquet. The novel
ends with Ward on the bridge of a ship, giving the command to sail
due North.

Lloyd, however, does differ from Travis. Both Travis and Condy
were departing for New York. The coming of love had not changed
the plans of the New Woman to pursue an "occupation." Feminist
historians thus have reason to give *Blix* special attention. For Lloyd,
however, the pattern is reversed. In chapter 9, Ward displays his
newly developed sensitivity as a disinterested lover by asking Lloyd
about *her* plans: "It would be very selfish of me to ask you to give up
your work. It's your life-work, your profession, your career." For
some reason both Lloyd and he view marriage as precluding the con-
tinuance of her career. Lloyd picks up a letter requesting her services
and tears it in two: " 'That, for my life-work,' said Lloyd Searight" *(W,*
235). Norris then further elevates this gesture to a manifestation of
high nobility, assigning Lloyd a new kind of heroic stature: "Lloyd's
discontinuance of her life-work had been in the nature of heroic
subjugation of self" *(W,* 241-42). Egotism is thus immolated on the
altar of love, as is the innovative concept of ideal womanhood offered in *Blix.* It does not reappear in the Norris canon.

A Man's Woman *as Autobiography*

The reason for this about-face appears to lie in the fact that, since
the composition of *Blix,* things had changed in Norris's relationship
with Jeannette. By the time of their engagement in July 1899, Jeannette had made a choice that Norris appreciated mightily, and he
revised his image of the ideal woman accordingly. With Norris's en-
couragement, Jeannette had been planning, as she explained to
Franklin Walker, to begin training in nursing. But, marriage looming
before her, it was necessary to deal with the particulars of the immediate future. Although she had made inquiries about a course of
study at San Francisco's Children's Hospital, her husband's position
was in New York, and Jeannette decided not to follow Travis's path,
opting instead for marriage without a career. Indeed, after their

wedding, it turned out that the only career she knew was her husband's, in which she was fully involved. Thus one kind of "man's woman" in *Blix* was keyed to Jeannette in 1897-98; another, more traditional kind influenced the conclusion of *A Man's Woman*, which celebrates Jeannette's self-sacrificing decision.

The Return to "Naturalism"

No matter how endearing a testimony to his fiancée, *A Man's Woman* is Norris's least successful novel. Dissatisfied with it himself, he was clearly relieved to turn to *The Octopus* and to the regaining of face with "The Epic of the Wheat" trilogy. He knew that he had faltered. But, while expressing regret to Isaac F. Marcosson on 22 November 1899, he also proclaimed his renewed enthusiasm: "I am going back *definitely* now to the style of [*McTeague*] and stay with it right along. I've been sort of feeling my way ever since the 'Moran' days and getting a twist of myself. Now I think I know where I am at and what game I play the best. The Wheat series will be straight naturalism with all the guts I can get into it" (*Letters*, 92-93). Thus he turned to *The Octopus* and *The Pit*, wherein the themes of sensitivity to the needs of others and the positive value of a "subjugation of self" would be developed with considerably more sophistication.

Chapter Six

The Epic of the Wheat:
The Octopus

In February 1900, when *A Man's Woman* was published after two newspaper serializations, *The Octopus* was assuming its shape. By then, Norris had been a reader for the new firm of Doubleday, Page & Co. for more than a month, and he was dividing his time between others' manuscripts and his own – as well as giving attention to Jeannette Black, whom he had married on 12 February. The previous April he had gone to San Francisco and the San Joaquin Valley to research the new novel; to develop a feel for the setting, he stayed at a ranch near Hollister that summer. The writing then proceeded slowly in New York, but from the house he had recently rented in Roselle, New Jersey, Norris was finally able to inform Isaac F. Marcosson on 13 September 1900 that "The Squid is nearing conclusion" (*Letters*, 123-24). And yet Doubleday did not advertise it as available until 30 March 1901, two years after its inception.

"The Squid" had developed an enormous gut, its 652 pages dwarfing *McTeague* and the soon-to-be-written *Pit*. Size alone was not the reason for the lengthy period of composition, though: the complex elaborations of the main plot, the large cast of characters, and the perplexing ethical and socioeconomic questions raised by the story based on California history made considerable demands on Norris. It is a difficult novel to summarize succinctly; nor does Norris's point of view allow a simple description either, for, as with the question of whether instinct is good *or* evil in *Vandover*, he again focused on complexities that did not invite absolute judgments.

The Historical Background: Norris's Analysis

While Norris updates events, incorporating allusions to San Francisco's 1894 Mid-Winter Fair and the 1897 famine in India, the story
was developed from his research concerning the Mussel Slough Affair of 1880 – a gun battle between wheat ranchers and representatives of the Southern Pacific railroad company that resulted from a
dispute over land in the San Joaquin Valley. The railroad had
attracted agriculturalists by advertising low-priced land ceded it by
the government; when the parcels were improved, the railroad hiked
its prices, surprising the growers who somewhat naively assumed
that advertisements constituted a legal contract. Violence attended
the serving of eviction notices. It was a prime example of the chi-
canery possible in a laissez-faire economy, wherein financial gain is
the ultimate standard by which everything is judged, even in the state
legislature and the courts. It was a perfect topic for a novelist given
to exposé writing.

Indeed, *The Octopus* was an early, prime example of Progressive
Era muckraking art.[1] It was, and is, a controversial one as well, for
Norris did not reduce the situation treated to an evil-trust versus
good-wheat-ranchers melodrama. Like John Steinbeck in *In Dubious
Battle* (1936), Norris disturbed the political economists on the left
and the right via what he considered necessary ambivalences. The
victims of "the octopus," while pathetic, are not spotless. Rather, in
Norris's view, these profit-oriented individuals who exercise absolute
power over their ranch hands become increasingly similar to the
businessmen who abuse them. Norris does not romanticize them as
noble husbandmen of the soil but frankly depicts them as agri-busi-
nessmen struggling to prevail in a dog-eat-dog economic order. Thus
Norris created for himself the first complexity with which he had to
deal as he pictured human nature the way it is: to maintain a sympa-
thetic point of view toward the ranchers while, at the same time,
making it clear that their ethicality is not innately superior to that of
the railroaders who inevitably win because of their greater sophistication. All the principals who participate in this economic system
reveal feet of clay.

The second complexity – which also appears in the epic's next
volume, *The Pit* – derives from Norris's observation that, like it or
not, the corrupt and humanly destructive system making America the

world's "breadbasket" was one that *worked*. The trilogy to be completed by the never-written *The Wolf* was to show how the system inarguably wreaked havoc in all quarters, and yet the inhumane means just as undeniably served humane ends via the production and distribution of an essential foodstuff. Norris, then, planned to present a positive, macrocosmic perspective on the *whole* truth, without sanctioning the ignobility of the Social Darwinists and plain rapacity of the railroad and its agents as the hungry were fed. This point of view was, of course, informed by Norris's own experiences as one born to the patrician class, and it was reinforced by his association with the prorailroad editorialists of *The Wave*. He was uniquely suited to offer what he probably considered a more "balanced" picture than that in *Main-Travelled Roads* (1891), in which Hamlin Garland's Populist loyalties were dominant. Norris was neither a Populist nor a partisan of monopolists such as the darling of *Wave* editorialists, Southern Pacific head Collis P. Huntington. He assumed the difficult task of attempting a middle-ground stance.

The maintenance of a dual perspective on a bad system that produced good results came at a price. Since 1901, interpreters have repeatedly expressed exasperation over Norris's apparent fickleness in a novel acknowledging that good may be seen amidst evil.[2] They have also experimented with various interpretations that permit a more ideologically orthodox reading, generally to the effect that Norris discounted the negative and accentuated the positive as he finally embraced a cosmic optimism similar to those of the Transcendentalists and post-Darwinian evolutionary idealists.[3] The question of what was his personal response to the events pictured is a perennial topic for debate. It is thus of cardinal importance to note what the main story is.

The Main Plot

Shorn of its many embellishments, the main story of *The Octopus* is relatively simple. Early in book 1, the conflict between the ranchers and the railroad is delineated. S. Behrman, the local representative of the trust headed by Shelgrim in San Francisco, controls the means by which the wheat is shipped out of the valley and essentials are brought in: in effect, he governs the "ranch" that is the whole valley.

Magnus Derrick and his son Harran are typical of the ranchers who cultivate the enormous fields that they plan to purchase at some unspecified future date. The railroad's control is early apparent as Harran flies into a rage when he sees the ploughs they have ordered and immediately need to use standing idly on a side rail. They cannot be unloaded because the railroad's system is designed so that the maximum rate can be charged: they must proceed to San Francisco and then be shipped back, at the higher than necessary cost. The Derricks are trying to change the situation by legitimate means of persuasion. But they soon find that the state's railroad commission – in the trust's pocket – will not honor a petition for an advantageous rate schedule.

Other ranchers such as Osterman, Broderson, and Annixter recognize the pragmatic response: they must do as the trust has done, arrange for the election of their own handpicked representatives to the commission. Magnus Derrick is the obvious leader for the conspiracy but he demurs on principle, until the railroad announces its elevated price for his land and, as book 1 ends, he is forced to choose between ruination or corruption. Like the others, he opts for the expedient course. Once a '49er drawn to the possibilities of quick wealth in the gold mines, he intends to make his fortune from the golden fields of grain, as many another did in 1897 because of the strong international demand for wheat that year.

In book 2, the Rancher's League is betrayed by Magnus's other son, Lyman, a San Francisco lawyer with gubernatorial ambitions who has long been on the railroad's secret payroll. Annixter, Broderson, Osterman, and others are killed when the railroad begins to evict the ranchers. The corruption of Magnus and his coconspirators is revealed by a valley journalist, Genslinger, who is also a railroad stooge. They are driven off the land. The railroad has triumphed.

The Tragic Theme

The wheat grown, it is of course harvested. From the points of view of those making a profit and those who benefit from the availability of bread, the consequences are good. *The Octopus*, however, focuses mainly on the human debacle that, ironically, develops before the background of the vitalistic spectacle of dry seed "miraculously" springing to life. As the greening of the brown fields occurs, the blighting of the lives of the ranchers and those associated with them also proceeds apace. And thus the broadest theme developed in *The Octopus*: life's complexity is seen in the lamentable admixture of life and death in which the good made possible by nature is tainted by evil inevitably resulting from greed. Theoretically, the debacle need not have occurred; practically, though, the novel convincingly illustrates that, human nature being what it is, the outcome was predictable in fin de siècle America.

When the climax of the main story occurs, Norris makes clear his thematic intention as one who had chosen to steer a middle course between left- and right-wing ideologies. Seeing the proposal of specific remedies for the undeniable shortcomings of the economic system as beyond his ken, Norris responded not as a political economist to the issues crystallized in the fatal conflict between the ranchers and railroad but as a Humanistic artist.[4] Yes, the tentacles of "the octopus" grip all within reach; the monstrously bloated trust is an evil force that strangles all who resist its will. But Norris moves beyond that facile metaphor to focus instead on individuals on both sides who are in the grip of their shared mania for self-aggrandizement. As in classical tragedy rather than mere muckraking tracts, *The Octopus* offers clarification of the fact that the problem lies neither in the stars nor in special-interest groups per se, but in the characters of those who view the stars and originate the adversarial groups.

Before this theme emerges in the scene at Hooven's house following the gun battle, Norris has already shown that he was interested in moving beyond the simplistic terminologies available to him as – at best – an amateur political economist. The Dyke subplot is a case in point. Dyke first appears as a locomotive engineer who has been ruthlessly fired by the railroad, solely as a cost-cutting expedient. Such villainy is not the exclusive behavior of the railroad, however. For Dyke's experience pairs with that of a ranch foreman, Delaney. Annixter fires this especially capable hand solely because of jealousy: a dairymaid who has caught Annixter's eye, Hilma Tree, seems to like Delaney, and Annixter cannot cope with having a rival. But that the ranching bosses are not any less ignoble than the railroad's administrators is only one of two points that Norris intends as he moves beyond muckraking. Dyke is his means of finally rendering meaningless black-versus-white distinctions such as that between "labor" and "capital." Fired as a laborer, Dyke immediately becomes a capitalist as he speculates on the likelihood of higher market prices and constancy in shipping rates with a planting of hops. Like the railroaders and the ranchers, the "little man" too hopes to make a killing via this gamble. When the railroad plays the same game by raising the rates, because it can make its killing that way, Dyke goes berserk. One sympathizes, as he does with the aggrieved Delaney. But Dyke's irresponsibility in getting even with the railroad via a train holdup renders him a victim who victimizes others: his dependent mother and motherless daughter face a much worse plight than was necessary. Norris has replaced the "labor" and "capital" figure with a plainly pathetic one whose foibles are simply *human*.

The Dyke subplot is not Norris's occasion to indulge in blaming a character who should have thought through more carefully the consequences of his actions – although, ideally, misery would have been lessened had he done so. Rather, his characterization is a minor example of what Norris saw as an essential feature of Zolaesque Naturalism: things are "twisted from the ordinary, wrenched out from the quiet, uneventful round of every-day life, and flung into the throes of a vast and terrible drama that works itself out in unleashed passion, in blood, and sudden death."[5] Life escapes our control, particularly when an irrational thirst for revenge, money, or other means for displaying and exercising power overcomes a Dyke or characters like Annixter who share Dyke's self- and socially destructive experience. In the midst of onrushing events, we do not recognize, or we forget, what is *really* important in the final analysis, and the results are calamitous.

The point regarding displaced values was ironically touched on in *McTeague* when Trina reflects on Zerkow's cutting Maria's throat, "And all this . . . on account of a set of gold dishes that never existed" (*Mc*, 321). She is amazed at how people complicate their lives, yet she suffers a similar fate for gold that *does* exist. Such mistakes in judgment abound in the Norris canon, and the self-aggrandizing foes of *The Octopus* come to the same end as Trina and McTeague in a struggle over the wheat – which suddenly appears worth no more than a mess of pottage in the face of agony, death, and bereavement.

After the firing has ceased, the dead and dying are brought together in Hooven's house. The portrait is of ever-vulnerable, frail humanity as Annixter's corpse is laid out and Annie Derrick discovers her slain son, Harran. Osterman's wound will prove fatal; Hooven, Dabney, and Broderson are dead. On the railroad's side, Delaney and Christian have also perished. And *The Octopus* will continue to depict the bitter harvest: Magnus becomes mentally enfeebled; Annixter's traumatized wife, Hilma, loses the child she is carrying; Presley, the poet visiting Magnus's ranch, becomes mentally unstable as he slips into profound depression and then leaps to manic optimism; and Hooven's daughter turns to prostitution in order to survive, as her mother succumbs to starvation in San Francisco.

Thematically, the most significant development in this key scene is the behavior of both the ranchers and the railroaders in Hooven's house. Once only in this novel, the Social Darwinist's "law" of competition, while an explanation of *how* such developments eventuate, appears irrelevant as humane values replace economic ones. Here Norris invites us to infer that traditional "higher values" apropos human and humane nature are still relevant to the modern world, no matter how redefined by scientists and social theorists, for even the novel's archvillain, S. Behrman, proves capable of sensitivity to what were once celebrated as humane values when *the* elemental experiences of pain and death are forced on his attention. For the moment he, like all of the other economic combatants, *cares*: "The surviving members of both Leaguers and deputies – the warring factions of the Railroad and the People – mingled together now with no thought of hostility. Presley helped the doctor to cover Christian's body. S. Behrman and Ruggles held bowls of water while Osterman was attended to. The horror of that dreadful business had driven all other considerations from the mind. The sworn foes of the last hour had no thought of anything but to care for those whom, in their fury, they had shot down."[6] It had to come to this before attention was paid to the essential. As in Crane's "The Open Boat," death reduces all to limpid simplicity. As in tragedy defined by Aristotle, intellectual clarification regarding what is truly important in the last analysis is proffered to the observer of the spectacle who would reflect on its significance.

Other Views on the Main Theme

This scene has not been traditionally identified as the key one in *The Octopus*. Rather, more attention has been given to that in which a speech by the railroad's head, Shelgrim, is delivered to Presley.[7] He views the debacle in rigidly deterministic terms, emphasizing natural forces and their manifestations in the economic order as laws dictated by the iron necessities of supply and demand. "Blame conditions, not men" (*O*, 576) is his apologia for what he, in fact, is personally responsible for having effected. Even more emphasis has been placed on another scene in which the viewpoint of a visionary shepherd, Vanamee, is expressed.[8] He is the hero of a wildly romantic subplot that is minimally connected to the main story. His problem has little to do with the economic warfare in the valley: years previously his lover, Angéle, was raped and murdered, and he is coping with his private affliction in a manner recalling those devised by several of Edgar Allan Poe's narrators. Falling in love with Angéle, Jr., he embraces the happy delusion that Angéle, Sr., did not *really* die. Furthermore, he proclaims to Presley, such evils as death and even evil itself are only illusory. He is able to echo not only Emerson but Alexander Pope, to the effect that, in the larger view, all is perfect in the universe (*O*, 634-39).

Reviewers of *The Octopus* were outraged to conclude that Shelgrim's speech seemed to be Norris's justification for the trust's behavior.[9] Later interpreters have read Vanamee's Orphic pronouncements as Norris's dramatic revelation of a Transcendentalism, or evolution-based philosophical idealism, that was his by 1901.[10] And thus the scene at Hooven's is of secondary importance – a melancholic moment superseded by vibrant optimism at the novel's end.

The conclusion of *The Octopus* is repeatedly cited by interpreters agreeing with Warren French that Norris showed himself an optimistic idealist – although the point of view rendered there is that of the character Presley rather than Norris.[11] A poet who has been searching since the first chapter for a vision of life in the West that he might articulate in hexameters, Presley finally finds the means to that end, as well as to escaping the depression that has plagued him since the death of his best friend, Annixter. He synthesizes both Shelgrim's and Vanamee's teachings, although it is the latter's vision that predominates:

> Men – motes in the sunshine – perished, were shot down in the very noon of life, hearts were broken, little children started in life lamentably handicapped; young girls were brought to a life of shame; old women died in the heart of life for lack of food. In that little, isolated group of human insects, misery, death, and anguish spun like a wheel of fire.
>
> *But the* WHEAT *remained* . . . that mighty world-force, that nourisher of nations, wrapped in Nirvanic calm, indifferent to the human swarm . . . moved onward in its appointed grooves. Through the welter of blood at the irrigation ditch . . . the great harvest . . . rolled like a flood from the Sierras to the Himalayas to feed thousands of starving scarecrows on the barren plains of India. (*O*, 651)

Presley has these thoughts on the deck of a ship off the California coast, beginning a cruise to regain his health. In its hold is the wheat that will feed the Indians. In his view this compensates for and then cancels the significance of *how* the wheat moved onward in its predetermined course, crushing some "human insects." And that there are "appointed grooves" in place argues, according to the teleological, evolutionary optimism espoused, that the natural system is *designed* thus – apparently by God – as good. Do we get a drift not discernible in any of Norris's previous novels? There is nothing but good, good, good – once the Annixter factor is put in proper perspective by Presley: "Falseness dies; injustice and oppression in the end of everything fade and vanish away. Greed, cruelty, selfishness, and inhumanity are short-lived; the individual suffers, but the race goes on. Annixter dies, but in a far distant corner of the world a thousand lives are saved. The larger view always and through all shams, all wickednesses, discovers the Truth that will, in the end, prevail, and all things, surely, inevitably, resistlessly work together for good" (*O*, 651-52).

That Norris's use of free indirect discourse here is problematic for modern readers is clear in critical commentary. Nor did his contemporaries see it used successfully: they too were puzzled to find tragedy seemingly perverted to tragicomic ends by Norris via Vanamee and then Presley. Further complicating the problem for those familiar with Norris's personality is the fact that he invites an autobiographical interpretation of Presley by assigning him some of his attitudes. For example, early in the novel Presley seems as hostile to aestheticism as Norris was in "An Opening for Novelists" when, in 1897, he attacked the "toy magazine" poets that are Presley's bane.

A problem in identifying Norris with Presley, though, is that Presley himself proves the effeminate, ineffectual, dilettantish poetaster identified in "An Opening for Novelists."[12] In the main story where the flawed but uniformly more vigorous males are actively engaged by physically and psychologically demanding tasks, Presley is – after Vanamee – the least involved figure. He putters with a poem while they struggle for their survival. He is an onlooker, essentially a flaneur like the trifling, failed artist Vandover. When not searching for "inspiration," he merely listens – cat in lap and smoking innumerable cigarettes – to the ranchers' discussions. He then serves as messenger for the principals. His one success in art, the poem "The Toilers," is correctly identified by Shelgrim as a plagiarism of Millet's painting of the economically downtrodden – Norris's shot at Edwin Markham's commercially successful "The Man with the Hoe" (1899). Indeed, it was a rather obvious shot because "The Toilers" is an actual poem in *The Man with the Hoe and Other Poems* (1899), which was published by Norris's own firm, Doubleday & McClure. Presley is also a failure as a would-be Populist orator because plain people cannot understand his literary allusions. He next fails during a brief stint as an anarchist, missing S. Behrman with the bomb he throws. *Bungler* is the term Norris chooses for Presley when preparing the reader to recognize the scene at Hooven's, rather than the conclusion of *The Octopus*, as the distinctly non-Transcendental apex of thematic development.

The Positive Framework for the Tragic Theme

For *The Octopus* or any literary work to be tragic, it must at least imply a positive standard for personality and behavior that was possible and that the hero failed to either achieve or maintain. Magnus might have been like the noble Roman republican leader type whom he physically resembles. Vanamee might have rationally accepted the fact of death. Presley might have become more like Annixter, who, not coincidentally, happens to be the only character who has something in common with the positively conceived heroes of *Blix* and *A Man's Woman*.

One of *Presley's* reflections elevates Annixter above all the novel's other males. Well before "there had come to Presley a deep-rooted suspicion that he was – of all human beings, the most wretched – a failure" (*O*, 567), Presley had arrived at a similar conclusion when measuring himself against Annixter. As Annixter expresses in his unpolished way the cogent new philosophy of life that he has developed since his marriage to Hilma Tree, Presley is beside himself with admiration and then crestfallen to discover his own inferiority to this diamond in the rough: "Beside [Annixter's] blundering struggle to do right, to help his fellows, Presley's own vague schemes, glittering systems of reconstruction, collapsed to ruin, and he himself, with all his refinement, with all his poetry, culture, and education, stood, a bungler at the world's workbench" (*O*, 468).

We may ask, At what has the intellectual failed, while this cowboy farmer blundered his way into a coherent view of things? It happens that Annixter has embodied in his behavior and conceptualized the value system that informs Norris's treatment of the scene in Hooven's house. As S. Behrman briefly demonstrates a neighborly, even brotherly, response – his "better self," we might term it – the behavior recalled is that of the meanest, most cantankerous, and least social of the wheat barons, Annixter, who had learned a better way to live. When Hilma fled this self-centered lecher who would "keep" rather than love her, and when Annixter concluded after the rejection of his satyrlike advances that he had unwittingly fallen in love, a major change in his personality was wrought – the kind of love in question being typed by Norris as disinterested rather than selfish. The Greco-Christian ideal of *agape* thus manifests itself, as does its paradoxical effect: that, by caring for the welfare of another rather than for ourselves, we obtain a kind of fulfillment unavailable to the self-server. Happiness is found in making the loved one happy, as is the case in *A Man's Woman* when Lloyd subjugates "self" for the sake of Ward. A healthy maturation is also an effect when self-centeredness is transcended – as the heroine of *The Pit* will discover. Personal gain is no longer the be-all and end-all of life.

As was the case with scatterbrained Condy Rivers, Annixter – the prune-eating nervous wreck who clenches his teeth even when

sleeping – levels out when Hilma gives a purpose to, even becomes
the main purpose of, his life. Psychologically, he is much more focused. There are socialization consequences as well, as not only the
misogynist turns lover but the misanthrope displays a philanthropy
equalled by none of the other characters. Norris had lightly touched
on this last notion in *Blix*, when Condy discovered that he had fallen
in love: he felt "a tenderness not for her only, but for all the good
things of the world" (*B*, 249). Here that sensitivity is expanded beyond interpersonal love *à deux* to become the experiential basis for
a social ethic.

   Well before Presley notes the change in Annixter, Hilma observes
and succinctly explains the significance of his unprecedented
decision to care for Mrs. Dyke and young Sidney when foreclosure
on Dyke's property is imminent:

> "You wouldn't have thought of being kind to [them] a little while ago. You
> wouldn't have thought of them at all. But you did now, and it's just because
> you love me true, isn't it? Isn't it? And because it's made you a better
> man. . . ."
>   "You bet it is, Hilma," he told her. (*O*, 435)

Presley then observes the same, summarizing the metamorphosis that
has occurred: "There was a time when you would have let them all
go to grass, and never so much as thought of them" (*O*, 467).

   In Annixter's following explanation, the positive theme of *The
Octopus*, as well as the "what might have been" notion informing the
scene at Hooven's, are crystallized:

> I was a machine before, and if another man, or woman, or child got in my way,
> I rode 'em down, and I never *dreamed* of anybody else. . . . But as soon as I
> woke up to the fact that I really loved [Hilma], why, it was glory hallelujah all
> in a minute, and, in a way, I kind of loved everybody then, and wanted to be
> everybody's friend. And I began to see that a fellow can't live *for* himself any
> more than he can live *by* himself. He's got to think of others. If he's got
> brains, he's got to think for the poor ducks that haven't 'em, and not give 'em
> a boot in the backsides because they happen to be stupid. . . . I've got a whole
> lot of ideas since I began to love Hilma, and just as soon as I can, I'm going to
> get in and *help* people. . . . That ain't much of a religion, but it's the best I've
> got, and Henry Ward Beecher couldn't do any more than that. (*O*, 467-68)

It is here that Presley judges himself a "bungler at the world's workbench." It is also here that Norris grounds a theme – one that might otherwise be perceived as sentimental Christian idealism – in a down-to-earth reality of the kind Vanamee's and Presley's *weltan-schauüngen* lack, for Norris had a common man, rather than an intellectual or visionary, articulate his key concept.[13] Then he capped the credibility generated thus by maintaining Annixter's "imperfect" status. Annixter has come a long way, but he does not messianically extend his discovery of the better way to live beyond the microcosm of his small community; tragically, the competitive side of his nature assumes dominance again as he is caught once more in the macrocosmic sequence of events carrying him and the other league members to their deaths. Like Dyke, he forgets what is truly important: his wife is widowed and his unborn child put in jeopardy as proprietary concerns replace personal values.

The social ethic Annixter represented – none other than the Judeo-Christian familiar to Norris's turn-of-the-century readers – is thus the value-specific framework for measuring the tragic loss of the possibility for amelioration of relations between men in the San Joaquin Valley. What is even more pathetic is that none of Norris's characters appears to have learned anything after the immediate show of mutual concern at Hooven's has ended. Behrman makes preparations for selling Magnus's grain. Shelgrim delivers his self-exculpating speech to Presley, insisting that this is the way things have to be. Presley has derived nothing from Annixter's example, instead becoming Vanamee's disciple. The lion will not lie down with the lamb in the San Joaquin Valley in the near future.

Norris's Maturation and Celebrity Status

Remarkable in *The Octopus* is how traditional Norris was becoming in his thought as he turned 30. In 1897, "The Puppets and the Puppy" anticipated the portraits of a godless world in *Moran*, *McTeague*, and particularly *Vandover*; the 1897 version of "Miracle Joyeux" is a story in which a Jesus with profound insight into human nature uses the same to blind two scoundrels.[14] With *The Octopus*, however, the positive values articulated are those of the Sermon on the Mount. It appears that the angry young iconoclast was mellowing the way Annixter did: a happily married man with his career in order, he had again celebrated in Hilma another ideal woman like Jeannette.

He was also beginning to develop an avuncular, if not paternal, tone of voice as he began to exercise an authority not previously granted him. In 1901, opportunities to write as an expert on American literature and culture were suddenly offered him. Concentrating on his novels and his work for S. S. McClure and then Frank N. Doubleday, Norris had not reviewed a book or a written a literary essay since 1898. When *The Octopus* replaced *A Man's Woman* as his best-selling book and established his image as a *very* serious writer who had focused on important socioeconomic matters, he was suddenly in demand as an expert. On 25 May 1901, his "Literature in the East" appeared in the *American Art and Literary Review*, and through 31 August this section of the Chicago *American* newspaper included "Frank Norris' Weekly Letter." He was an "insider" to the New York literary establishment, and most of these essays consisted of shoptalk about how the literary trade *really* works. The 3 August "Letter," however, was special: in it he gave his fullest and last definition of Naturalism as a synthesis of Realism and Romanticism of the kind seen in *The Octopus*.[15]

He was next engaged by the *Boston Evening Transcript* in November, continuing to provide behind-the-scenes reflections on publishing in pieces such as "Why Women Should Write the Best Novels; and Why They Don't" and "Retail Bookseller: Literary Dictator." In 1901, he also wrote essays of a more exalted kind for the Chicago-based, reform-minded *World's Work*. Its progressive readership required high seriousness, and the truth-telling author of *The Octopus* provided veritable sermons on the high calling of the artist: "The True Reward of the Novelist" and "The Need of a Literary Conscience" made it clear that Victorian earnestness had not perished before the assaults of Oscar Wilde or Gelett Burgess. In these and several 1902 essays posthumously collected in *The Responsibilities of the Novelist*, a Norris who had donned the mantle of social responsibility stood forth sincerely enunciating a credo emphasizing the need to tell the truth at all costs.[16]

In 1901, he also returned to short fiction, rewriting *Yvernelle* as a prose romance entitled "The Riding of Felipe." That he had not lost his sense of humor was apparent in "Buldy Jones, *Chef de*

Claque." Finally, it was clear that he remained loyal to the cultural tradition in which he had been reared by Gertrude Norris. On 18 December, the author of the gothic Vanamee subplot of *The Octopus* paid homage to the school to which he was still loyal: "A Plea for Romantic Fiction."[17] Entering his maturity, Norris remained a writer and thinker destined to perplex interpreters who would balk before the prospect of a romance writer with the vision of a critical Realist, despite the precedents set by Zola and the "Romantic" story line developed by Flaubert in *Madame Bovary*. In fact, as Norris praised "Romantic Fiction," he was writing a novel in the Romantic-Realistic style that he termed *Naturalism*. *The Pit* was Norris's final spirited, yet sober, delineation of the way in which environment can warp the personality of an individual as she is "flung into the throes of a vast and terrible drama."

Chapter Seven

The Epic of the Wheat: *The Pit*

During February and March 1901, as type was being set for *The Octopus*, Frank and Jeannette Norris were in Chicago researching the second volume of his trilogy, *The Pit*. After a visit to California and a vacation at Greenwood Lake, New Jersey, that spring and summer, he was writing in earnest in September, just before they returned to New York City. In addition, he continued composing literary essays for newspapers and magazines, as well as short stories (43 such items appeared between 1902 and 1903). Still employed as a manuscript reader by Doubleday, Page & Co., this sole bread-winner – whose daughter was born on 9 February 1902 – put himself under considerable pressure. When he finished the manuscript of *The Pit* in June 1902, he had finally succeeded in reaching his goal: being a professional writer free from the editorial work that began with *The Wave*, continued with the S. S. McClure organization, and extended itself into his relationship with Doubleday, Page & Co. On 22 July 1902, confident that he could earn his way as a self-supporting fiction writer, he left New York for San Francisco, reestablishing his residence there. The serialization of an abbreviated version of *The Pit* in the *Saturday Evening Post* would begin in September.

The future appeared bright, and in *The Pit* this showed. It is one of the few novels in the Naturalistic tradition that features a happy ending. Unlike Presley in *The Octopus*, the character with the last word and final ruminations in this work has commonsensically come to terms with her own shortcomings – particularly her myopic self-centeredness. Again unlike Presley, Laura Dearborn Jadwin does not, at the end of *The Pit*, pontificate about the macrocosmic complexities of the socioeconomic order. She is merely perplexed by the destruction left in the wake of so good a thing as wheat as it moves eastward from the American midwest and west, through Chicago's

Board of Trade. She too has been touched by it, indirectly, because of her husband's obsession with wheat speculation. Curtis Jadwin is still recovering from the mental and emotional breakdown that his megalomaniacal quest to control the whole of American wheat precipitated.

A Heroine of Romance

For 10 of the 11 chapters of this *bildungsroman*, however, this heroine suffers mainly because of her immaturity: determined in her self-conception and behavior by the concepts and imagery generated by the Romantic culture in which she has come to physical maturity, her psychology is that of the heroine pictured in Gustave Flaubert's *Madame Bovary* (1857) and later in Kate Chopin's *The Awakening* (1899). Her personality is, literally, an aggregate of the traits of the Romantic heroines with whom she has vicariously identified in her reading and theatergoing: Shakespeare's Juliet and Marguerite of Gounod's opera *Faust*, for example. Like Emma Bovary who simple-mindedly lusts for the grand passion known by the heroine in a similar opera, *Lucia de Lammermoor*, and like Chopin's Edna Pontelier who becomes a thrall to the fantasy of having a love that will provide the sublime experience articulated in Frédéric Chopin's music, Laura pursues the impossible and becomes a victim of a reality that will not conform to her expectations of it.

When we first see her in the vestibule of Chicago's Auditorium Theatre, waiting for the remainder of her opera party to assemble, she resembles the plucky New Woman of the turn of the century, dauntlessly risking the impropriety of introducing herself to Curtis Jadwin, whom she knows is to be one of their number. She is hardly the wilting violet when, with the aplomb of a Blix, she approaches the real-estate baron as her equal. Once seated in the theater, though, she proves the girlish paradigm of the naive adolescent, defenseless before the intoxicating allure of ecstatic love experience represented in *Faust*: "She sat spell-bound, her hands clasped tight, her every faculty of attention at its highest pitch."[1] It is not long before the fantasy on stage becomes the stimulant of a vision of herself as a heroine of romance:

> She dreamed of another Laura, a better, gentler, more beautiful Laura, whom everybody, everybody loved dearly and tenderly, and who loved everybody, and who should die beautifully, gently, in some garden far away – die because of a great love – beautifully, gently in the midst of flowers, die of a broken heart, and all the world should be sorry for her, and would weep over her when they found her dead and beautiful in her garden, amid the flowers and the birds, in some far-off place, where it was always early morning and where there was soft music. (*P*, 21)

The embodiment of *weltschmerz*, Laura gives vent to her bitter-sweet melancholy as tears roll down her face, dropping on her white-gloved fingers. Norris's purple prose is perfectly suited to the fantasy-prone young lady who has emerged from the guise of a New Woman, and she is soon entertaining the equally irrational desire to "drift off into the past, far away, through rose-coloured mists and diaphanous veils." The free indirect discourse further reveals that she would like to leave the sordid modern world, "reclining in a silver skiff drawn by swans, to the gentle current of some smooth-flowing river that ran on forever and forever" (*P*, 22). When Marguerite sings her swoon-inducing aria of newfound ecstatic love, "He loves thee," Laura "seemed only to come to herself some five minutes later" (*P*, 23).[2]

Laura *is* Marguerite – and Juliet. She is also, later in her story, Thackeray's Ethel Newcome, Racine's Phèdre, Shakespeare's Lady Macbeth, Bizet's Carmen and a good many other fictional characters whose personalities she dons. She lacks what Norris describes in chapter 10 as an "identity" that is her own; who and what Laura is at particular moments typically involves a literary allusion. When she asserts herself, she does so by playing a role – from insouciant coquette to histrionic grande dame to pathetic victim – that promises a way of glamorously coping with the problematic situations she confronts; with increasing frequency, however, her role-playing either complicates her situation or, at best, postpones the inevitable need to deal directly with actualities not to her liking. Eventually pushed to the verge of psychosis, Laura is allowed by her creator to escape the "cruel cult of self" (*P*, 404) that is Romantic narcissism, but only after she has fully illustrated what, ironically, is manifestly obvious in much High Romantic art.

Here is the irony. Both Gounod's *Faust* and Shakespeare's *Romeo and Juliet* make it clear to the commonsensical that Romantic

Love renders one maladapted to the exigencies of life as it is. No impossible expectations and wild suffering, no Romantic Love. *The Pit* is Norris's exposé of not only the amoral machinations of the capitalists at the Chicago Board of Trade[3]; it is also his Zolaesque indictment of the whited sepulchre that is Romantic culture. The pernicious effects of both are dramatized throughout the novel.

The second chapter makes it clear that Laura typically does not focus on the negative dimensions of Romantic experience. At the opera she paid no attention to *Faust*'s grisly fourth and fifth acts, wherein the price for mindless surrender to passion is paid. Marguerite, impregnated by Faust, is abandoned by him; her brother Valentine curses her on discovering her condition, and he dies at the hands of Faust and Mephistopheles; Marguerite kills her child and is cast into prison. As with Juliet, things do not work out well, despite the grandeur of love's coming. Laura, however, must learn this lesson on her own; now she only looks forward to the high gratification that will someday come to her. Her recent move from puritanical Barrington, Massachusetts, to Chicago appears to bring her closer to the fulfillment of her dreams. Indeed, she is already faring better than Marguerite or Juliet: now that Curtis Jadwin has entered her life to join Landry Court and Sheldon Corthell, she will have three Fausts in tow, each positively dying to obtain her hand: "Life never had seemed half so delightful. Romantic, she felt Romance, unseen, intangible, at work all about her. And love, which of all things knowable was dearest to her, came to her unsought." The chapter ends with Laura speaking to herself: "I think that I am going to be very happy here" (*P*, 77). Romance, however, brings her anything but contentment.

The Knight in a Business Suit

With Laura positioned thus to be, as Norris explained in a letter to Isaac F. Marcosson, the central figure to which all relates in *The Pit*, her future husband is more fully introduced in the third chapter (*Letters*, 173). Curtis is a country boy who came to Chicago for the resolute pursuit of the American Dream. He has made a killing in real-estate ventures and, still a young man, is the verification of the Franklinesque success myth.

The great bourgeois would seem to have little in common with
the aesthetically oriented Laura who has long hoped to become an
actress, a great tragedienne like Modjeska, but we soon note that
they are similar in one respect. Curtis possesses visionary propensi-
ties as grandiose and dynamic as those displayed by Laura at the
opera. On his way to the office of his broker, Sam Gretry, in the
Board of Trade building, he pauses to reflect on this locale of the pit
where commodities like wheat are traded: "Often Jadwin had noted
the scene, and, unimaginative though he was, had long since conceived the notion of some great, some resistless force within . . . that
held the tide of the streets within its grip, alternately drawing it in
and throwing it forth" (*P*, 79). As he stands there elaborating this initial image, he eventually elevates his conceit to a cosmic drama of
Melvillean proportions:

> There in the centre of the Nation, midmost of that continent that lay between
> the oceans of the New World and the Old, in the heart's heart of the affairs of
> men, roared and rumbled the Pit. It was as if the Wheat, Nourisher of the Na-
> tions, as it rolled gigantic and majestic in a vast flood from West to East, here,
> like a Niagara, finding its flow impeded, burst suddenly into the appalling fury
> of the Maëlstrom, into the chaotic spasm of a world-force, a primeval energy,
> blood-brother of the earthquake and the glacier, raging and wrathful that its
> power should be braved by some pinch of human spawn that dared raise bar-
> riers across its courses. (*P*, 80)

Curtis reflects on the madness of those who have tried to corner
the wheat market, and yet he is one of the "human spawn" who
eventually tries to control this "chaotic spasm of a world-force." Like
Laura, he will try to make reality conform to his will and be broken in
the attempt the way she is. She will be the Romantic heroine by transcending the ordinary experiences had by commonplace women; he
will reveal his kinship to Captain Ahab and Jay Gatsby by testing his
mettle against the natural force symbolized by the wheat. In short,
The Pit is a variation on the theme and characterizations introduced
two years earlier in *A Man's Woman*.

The Course of "True Love"

The relationship between the two principals is initiated in earnest in
the next chapter, when, at a rehearsal for a charity play in which

Laura will play the lead, Curtis abruptly proposes marriage to this woman he barely knows, as the equally strong-willed and success-driven Ward Bennett did in *A Man's Woman*. The artiste Sheldon Corthell woos her as well shortly afterwards, and boyish Landry Court goes so far as to steal a kiss that same night. For the first time, Laura realizes the stresses that are a part of playing the loved one to three men at the same time; in a rage for having made herself so vulnerable, and chastising herself for having played the coquette by encouraging such advances, she decides to amend her ways. She dispatches three dismissals, and two do their job. The next day, the new, more proper Laura is learning a new role to play from John Ruskin's description of the ideal behavior of altruistic womanhood in the "Queen's Gardens" essay of *Sesame and Lilies*, when Curtis's card is brought to her (*P*, 145-46). Ruskin's point is that a woman finds her divinely intended fulfillment in serving the male who requires her aid to realize his potential for fulfillment, and Laura almost immediately has the opportunity to embrace the role offered in the essay by modeling the self-sacrifice of a Ruth. We begin to receive the impression that Norris, the anti-Romantic ideologue, is designing his plot to illustrate how, one by one, the roles Laura's culture encourages her to play are self-destructive.

This Faust of galvanic willpower is unfamiliar with failure and sees Laura's dismissal as merely an obstacle to overcome; in the manner of the hero in the Romantic Love tradition, he becomes madly devoted to Laura despite her frequent protestations that she does not love him. He pines, becomes physically ill, and demonstrates that his fervor is as unrelenting as it is burdensome.

Laura, unfortunately, cannot immediately bring herself to play her part in the scenario as his lover. For the second time, the "Romance" she thought she wanted complicates rather than elevates. Worse, the sympathy-inducing sufferings of the maniacally persistent Curtis eventually push her to the unthinkable: the motherly Ruskinesque heroine accepts *Curtis's* problem as her own; ridden by guilt, she gives her hand to the man she does not love. She "solves" the problem Vandover-style by taking the line of least resistance, halfheartedly playing Juliet to his Romeo and allowing the Romantic script, rather than her own feelings, to determine her behavior. It is a classic example of a Romantically informed superego overriding a weak ego, and the conflict between the two spells profound neurosis. She is alleviated of guilt. But, as Curtis triumphantly transcends depression, she falls prey to it. While satisfying Curtis's, her own needs have not been met, as she makes clear when telling Mrs. Cressler that she is not sure she loves Curtis: "'I thought when love came it was to be – oh, uplifting, something glorious like Juliet's love or Marguerite's. Something that would – ' Suddenly she struck her hand to her breast, her fingers shut tight, closing to a fist. 'Oh, something that would shake me all to pieces. I thought that was the only kind of love there was'" (*P*, 161). Despite her wild mood swings and strategies for redefining love, this remains Laura's dominant attitude until the final chapter of *The Pit*. She *will* have "the only kind of love" described here. It is the only kind she can imagine.

When her sister Page expresses shock on hearing that Laura does not love her fiancé, Laura adopts two roles to make the illogical seem rational. She astounds her by representing herself as a gold digger, interested only in the luxuries that Curtis can provide (*P*, 167). Then she images herself more graciously as a haughty princess who scorns the affections of her knight: "A man ought to love a woman more than she loves him. It ought to be enough for him if she lets him give her everything she wants in the world. He ought to serve her like the old knights – give up his whole life to satisfy some whim of hers; and it's her part, if she likes, to be cold and distant. That's my idea of love" (*P*, 168). These and other experiments in finding a satisfying storybook part to play do not work. Through two chapters, her intimates wonder at her growing introversion, nervousness, and sudden outbursts as the wedding day draws nearer. During the wedding ceremony she seems catatonic; she numbly honors her commitment, and then breaks down in her bedroom at home, when it is time to leave on her honeymoon and to consummate a nonexistent love.

The stress is too much for her and, true to the theory that Freud would later propound, hers is the experience of infantile regression. With no one to turn to for solace and wondering what had become of "the little black-haired girl of Barrington," she kneels at her bed before God, a gesture recalling Vandover's manifestation of his overwhelming sense of helplessness: "Her head in her folded arms, she prayed – prayed in the little unstudied words of her childhood, prayed that God would take care of her and make her a good girl; prayed that she might be happy; and prayed to God to help her in

her new life, and that she should be a good and loyal wife" (*P*, 187).
The answer to her prayer? Curtis is suddenly at her side, with con-
solation in his voice: "Dear, I understand, I understand." As in Christian fundamentalism, so in Romantic Love. She need only turn to her
savior, accept his love, and the tear will be wiped from her eye. Nat-
uralistically viewed, the psychological determinisms impinging on her
sweep her into his arms; Romantically viewed, Curtis is the hero who
will rescue her from distress. She capitulates, immediately rewriting
her role in her heretofore pathetic melodrama to accommodate a
tragicomic conclusion: "From the first I must have loved you without
knowing it" (*P*, 187). One may wonder which play, poem, or story
provided the prompt for Laura's spectacular metamorphosis.

Romantic Ecstasy

Three years pass, and chapter 6 reveals that Curtis is no longer the
Petrarchan gallant intoxicated by his Laura. His new stimulant is
wheat speculation and he is beginning to pursue the goddess of fortune as aggressively as he once did his wife. Speaking with Sam
Gretry about his dead sister Sadie and how he wishes he could now
use his wealth to make her happy, Curtis unintentionally brings
Laura into the conversation, at which point his tone changes:

> "Well," hazarded Gretry, "you've got a good wife in yonder to – "
> Jadwin interrupted him. He half turned away, thrusting his hands
> suddenly into his pockets. Partly to himself, partly to his friend he murmured:
> "You bet I have. . . . Oh, well, never mind," he murmured.
> Gretry, embarrassed, constrained, put his chin in the air, shutting his
> eyes in a knowing fashion.
> "I understand," he answered. "I understand, J." (*P*, 200-1)

The intimacy between the two men is not equalled when Curtis and
Laura are seen together.

The enormity of what occurred when Laura denied the past and
created a new present as she leaped to the belief that she had always
loved Curtis is not clear until her condition three years later is seen.
Her new personality is one oblivious to the fact that Curtis has become disaffected. Indeed, for her he is still the god who entered her

life that afternoon, and the imagery associated with him is that of
Isaiah, Revelation, and the hymn "Amazing Grace":

> A great fact had entered her world, a great new element, that dwarfed all
> other thoughts. . . . This was her love for her husband. It was as though until
> the time of her marriage she had walked in darkness, a darkness that she fan-
> cied was day; walked perversely, carelessly, and with a frivolity that was almost
> wicked. Then, suddenly, she had seen a great light. Love had entered her
> world. In her new heaven a new light was fixed, and all other things were
> seen only because of this light; all other things were touched by it, tempered
> by it, warmed and vivified by it. (*P*, 203)

She has apparently established the record for maintaining ecstasy in
the tradition of Romantic Love literature. After three years, Laura is
still enjoying the experience that was only momentary for Marguerite, though that soon ends.

In a passage in the *Saturday Evening Post* version of the novel,
Laura's bliss is even more apparent as she ruminates on the perfec-
tion of her life with Curtis:

> Never had an ugliness entered her gardens. In her arbors never a fruit grew
> dry. The fountains of her bowers never flowed with bitter waters. For her the
> asphodel flowered with a sweetness that never faded. For her strong walls,
> unbidden, rose to fence her from the harshness of the world. For her the
> wind was tempered. For her the flints of the pathways were soft with mosses.
> A queen, beautiful, excellent; a queen, crowned and adored, her days full of
> the breath of loving-kindness, she walked continually in green pastures and
> beside still waters, goodness and mercy in her train; in her eyes the radiance
> of a great love, and in her heart the Golden Secret of a perfect and untroubled
> joy.
>   Her husband she knew was no less happy.[4]

As the conversation between Curtis and Sam makes clear, the
"reality" of her "new heaven" is wholly mental and may recall
Vanamee's and Presley's visions of a world in which vicissitudes are
finally unreal and goodness alone prevails. Like the two visionaries of
The Octopus, Laura is living in a world other than that known by the
other characters.

Romantic Agony

When the disparity between the ideal and the real becomes so great that even Laura must recognize it, she returns to the stressful condition of her courtship and engagement: " 'Dear,' said Laura, finally, 'I'm seeing less and less of you every day, and I had so looked forward to this summer, when we were to be together all the time' " (*P*, 226). Addicted to the rush that comes with living in Juliet's balcony, Laura is finding it difficult to accept Curtis's growing preoccupation with business matters. He is becoming addicted to the high drama that is "the swirl of the great maelstrom in the Board of Trade Building," for "of late Jadwin's eye and ear were forever turning thitherward" (*P*, 226). Chapter 7 begins with what soon becomes Laura's refrain: "Curtis dear, . . . when is it all going to end – your speculating? . . . Last night, when Mr. Gretry was here, you said . . . that you would be all through your talk in an hour . . . I waited till eleven, and then I went to bed. Dear I – I – I was lonesome" (*P*, 230). His explanation is that he cannot help himself: "It's the fun of the thing; the excitement – " (*P*, 231). A proof of his new obsession is then given as he rushes out to do battle with his opponents at the Board:

> Laura sat thinking. At last she rose.
> "It is the first time," she said to herself, "that Curtis ever forgot to kiss me good-by." (*P*, 236)

The Pit is not a "novel of degeneration" in the style of *Vandover and the Brute* or Zola's *L'Assommoir*. Both the heroine and hero move from discontent to dementia, but the sustained, alternating portraits of their worsening psychological conditions (like those of Lloyd and Ward in *A Man's Woman*) make "novel of complication" the more appropriate description. As in the earlier novel, the plot becomes increasingly melodramatic. Laura's quest is to regain the ecstasy she has known for three years; Curtis's is to conquer and control American wheat the way he once brought Laura to heel.[5] The plot is further complicated by Laura being tempted to forget her wedding vows, as Curtis already has in pursuing the "bitch goddess of success."

Feeling spurned by Curtis, Laura takes a ride in Lincoln Park to collect her wits. Enter Sheldon Corthell who has returned to Chicago from Italy, having found that he cannot get over her. He is so fortunate as to find that Curtis has begun neglecting his wife. The seduction of Laura begins in earnest and with remarkable success: the aesthetic temperament of Laura has received little exercise during three year of marriage to a Philistine; aesthetic experience is the bait that the artiste expertly uses. Visiting Laura one evening, Corthell flatters Laura by treating her as a near-equal when discussing evolutionary philosophy and art.[6] Playing the organ for her, he adeptly manipulates her toward dalliance via the performance of three Romantic compositions of increasing intensity: one of Mendelssohn's *Songs without Words*, Beethoven's *Appassionata*, and then Liszt's *Mephisto Walzer*. As at the opera in chapter 1, Laura is aroused, and ecstasy returns: "Laura was transfixed, all but transported. . . . Music she understood with an intuitive quickness; and those prolonged chords of Liszt's, heavy and clogged and cloyed with passion, reached some hitherto untouched string within her heart, and with resistless power twanged it so that the vibration of it shook her entire being, and left her quivering and breathless, the tears in her eyes, her hand clasped till the knuckles whitened" (*P*, 250). It appears that Corthell has earned a quick victory, for Laura begins thinking of a new life – without Curtis. In the future she envisions, "Corthell should select her pictures, and should play to her from Liszt and Beethoven that music which evoked all the turbulent emotion, all the impetuosity and fire and exaltation that she felt was hers" (*P*, 251). At this juncture, however, Curtis returns home, and Laura is suddenly, and without self-consciousness, the devoted wife once more.

The villain of the piece is foiled, failing again and again. For Laura's Romantic expectations prove Curtis-specific, and, in a reversal of the roles seen during their courtship, Laura plays the pining lover, the "knight" who loves more than he is loved, through chapter 10. She also plays the part of the scorned woman, Racine's Phèdre, who will wreak her revenge on her Thésée. She tries as well to win his attention by performing a brief scene from Racine's *Athalie*, mimicking another femme fatale. Then in full costume, she is the whore with a heart of ice intending to tantalize her Don José, dancing before Curtis as Bizet's Carmen. Then, again, and alone as usual in the Jadwins' mansion, she is pining – profoundly depressed. Hope returns as Curtis promises to abandon the Board of Trade for home on the evening of her birthday. Laura's plan is to overwhelm him with her beauty and to subjugate him at last: "She felt the same pride in [her beauty] as the warrior in a finely tempered weapon." Laura "knew she would prevail" (*P*, 404).

The Napoleon of LaSalle Street

Analogous to this development is Curtis's behavior motivated by overweening ambition and hubrislike confidence in his invincibility, which has been growing by leaps and bounds since chapter 7, when he left home without kissing Laura. At the close of the same chapter, he becomes truly Napoleonic in his ambition. To control the wheat no longer seems madness to a man becoming increasingly mad:

> Jadwin sprang forward, gripping the broker by the shoulder.
> "Sam," he shouted, "do you know – great God! – do you know what this means? Sam, we can corner the market!" (*P*, 268)

Like Laura, he can subjugate anyone who dares defy his power: "He knew that he overtopped them all. . . . He was stronger, bigger, shrewder than them all" (*P*, 282-83). And he does corner the whole of May wheat – whereupon he decides that he can hold his corner into July. Sam Gretry protests the insanity of the risk. Curtis's mega-lomania is all too apparent in his response: "I'm watching this thing. You can't tell me anything about it. I've got it all figured out" (*P*, 346). Sam offers an insightful diagnosis: "Then you're the Lord Almighty himself."

He is not. Unable to sleep, fixated at every moment on the wheat, and experiencing both nervous spasms and mental lapses, he is breaking beneath the strain: "A dry pringling aura as of billions of minute electric shocks crept upward over his flesh, till it reached his head, where it seemed to culminate in a white flash, which he felt rather than saw" (*P*, 349). Despite the recurrence of such symptoms, he persists and cannot see clearly what is so apparent to Sam: with Curtis driving up the price by buying all the wheat on the market, the American farmers are, of course, giving more acreage to wheat that spring, and a huge surplus of grain does pour into the trading pit.

The "Great Bull" cannot buy it all to keep up the price at the level to which he has inflated it, and he is overwhelmed as the reports on the new harvest flood in:

> Jadwin was in the thick of confusion by now. And the avalanche, the undiked Ocean of Wheat, leaping to the lash of the hurricane, struck him fairly in the face.
>
> He heard it now, he heard nothing else. The Wheat had broken from his control. For months, he had, by the might of his single arm, held it back; but now it rose like the upbuilding of a colossal billow. It towered, towered, hung poised for an instant, and then, with a thunder as the grind and crash of chaotic worlds, broke upon him, burst through the Pit and raced past him, on and on to the eastward and to the hungry nations.
>
> And then, under the stress and violence of the hour, something snapped in his brain. (*P*, 392)

At approximately the same time, Laura, waiting for her prey at home, snaps as well. Feeling rejected once more, she flies into a rage: "All the passion of the woman scorned shook her from head to foot. At the very moment of her triumph she had been flouted, in the pitch of her pride!" (*P*, 406). Hearing steps, she is overjoyed to think that her lover has returned at last – only to find that it is instead Corthell come to bring her a birthday present. A greater snapping then occurs, for Laura becomes incoherent as Corthell once again asks her to run away with him. With tears in his eyes, Corthell – for the first time forgetting himself and his plan for self-gratification – sounds a genuine note of sympathy: "God forgive whoever – whatever has brought you to this pass" (*P*, 410).[7]

Corthell slithers from the mansion as Curtis stumbles in, emotionally devastated and mentally enfeebled. Laura, as incapacitated, "groped her way toward him, her heart beating, the tears streaming down her face." Being the heroine of a tragic romance in real life or the hero of an adventure tale with a gut-rending finale has not been easy: "Together they made their way to the divan, and sank down upon it side by side, holding to each other, trembling and fearful, like children in the night" (*P*, 411).

The Triumph of Realism

The conclusion reads very much like an epilogue, for both the quest for ideal love and the battle with the earth itself are over. Significant is the absence of Romantic imagery in this one chapter; noteworthy as well is the commonsensical behavior of the erstwhile grand figures who have been whittled down to normal proportions by experience. Curtis has been bedridden for weeks and is now largely recuperated from his malaise. Laura has been his constant companion and has sent Corthell packing. In their conversations, she has also made full disclosure of the "affair" to Curtis – who blames himself for what she has been through. Neither is exacting the pound of flesh from the other. Curtis sounds one of the themes: "I fancy we both have been living according to a wrong notion of things" (P, 417). Laura too signals the emergence of a new perspective when paraphrasing Milton in Book 12 of *Paradise Lost*: " 'The world is all before us where to choose' " (P, 414). Milton's emphasis was on the responsible use of freedom, and Laura is delighted to have the opportunity to begin anew with Curtis in cultivating the less Romantic but more meaningful personal bonding that has resulted from sharing the experience of adversity. To echo Milton once more, theirs has been a fortunate fall; both seem to be able to see things as they actually are and to be able to deal with them in a truly rational manner. They are preparing to leave Chicago for the West, American archetypes looking for the fresh start not enjoyed by their models, the bourgeois B. F. Norris and prima donna Gertrude Doggett Norris.

Never the Pollyanna, Norris closed *The Pit* by qualifying the halcyon tone of the conclusion and restating the imagery linking the second volume of the wheat trilogy to *The Octopus* and the next one, *The Wolf*. On their way to the train station, Laura looks out the cab window to see her husband's onetime nemesis, "the pile of the Board of Trade building, black, monolithic, crouching on its foundations like a monstrous sphinx with blind eyes – crouching there without a sound, without a sign of life, under the night and the drifting veil of rain" (P, 421). As with Annixter in *The Octopus*, the microcosm of personal relationships has finally proven manageable and a source of positive experience. The macrocosm of the socio-economic condition in the world of laissez-faire capitalism is another matter. Neither Norris nor his heroine seems to have a clue as to how one would bring such forces under control.

Given the descriptions of the wheat as symbol of the congeries of forces both contained within and having an impact on society, it is unlikely that Norris would have developed in the never written *Wolf* a transcendent viewpoint allowing him to explain away the unruly, unpredictable, and inhumane aspects of international trade in essential commodities. Emerson might have seen through the hurly-burly a heart-gladdening principle of benign unity in the 1840s; at the turn of the century, however, neither Norris nor Henry Adams nor Stephen Crane could. Instead, as in his previous novels, Norris focused in *The Pit* on what he could understand and saw as remediable. When Laura is forced to look beyond herself in concern for her seriously ill husband, Norris pictures her as having found her way out of "the cruel cult of self," which might gratify only a masochist. When Curtis is driven out of the pit a broken man, he is forcefully liberated from self-absorption because he needs help from another. Norris, the Humanist who used Naturalistic literary methods, understood such matters. Indeed, they inform his canon from beginning to end.

Conclusion

Summarizing Frank Norris's career is a simple matter if one is intent on radical reductionism for the sake of getting to the "heart" of his canon. He was a Literary Naturalist dedicated to demonstrating that heredity and environment, complicated by chance developments, determine character, experience, and the shape of one's life. The problem with this truism, however, is that Norris and all other authors now thought of as Naturalistic did and do not limit themselves to such a facile updating of the antique Greco-Roman concept of fate. Dreiser did not fix his identity thus in *Sister Carrie* (1900); no work by Stephen Crane allows the reader the luxury of reducing him to a sentence. The variety one finds in the Norris canon will first be seen in works so different as *McTeague* and *The Octopus* – both of which Norris conceived of as Naturalistic. The similarities between *The Octopus* and *The Pit* are Zolaesque: both depict individuals whose lives have escaped their control and have become grotesquely warped by the impact of drives and forces, but *The Pit*, especially, eschews the idea of an iron law of necessity. For it is noteworthy that a character so weak as Laura Jadwin is able to regain control of her life and develop an apparently workable means to achieving real felicity. Vandover perishes; Laura makes an effort to change and succeeds, as does Condy Rivers in *Blix*.

Norris is, indeed, most appropriately remembered as a Literary Naturalist – but only if one expands his definition of Naturalism the way Donald Pizer has, to see the school as within the great Humanistic tradition, rather than as a scientistic, or pseudoscientific, aberration in an age of positivism.[1] Neither Naturalism nor Norris can be envisioned as in a cul de sac, a momentary divergence from ongoing scrutiny of the human condition initiated in the Renaissance. Who and what are we? Where are we going? The question posed by Norris's contemporary, Paul Gaugin, echoes Thomas More, Desiderius Erasmus, François Rabelais, and Shakespeare. It is Norris's question too, as much as it was Emile Zola's.

Norris's canon, though, is not always so grandly serious. His impressionistic visual flourishes are often no more intellectually significant than the idea-free paintings of Claude Monet and Auguste Renoir. Like them, he takes pleasure in his art as he gives it to us. His comic writing is frequently gratuitous, particularly when he indulges in black humor.[2] His delight in parody and satire – which he shares with Zola – should not be overlooked: in *Moran* he hoisted the adventure-romance genre on its own petard, and we should note his playfulness in *The Pit* as well. Laura wants romance, just as Norris's envisioned reader for *Moran* demanded it. Norris gave the *Moran* readership what it wanted, with a vengeance. Laura is given both Romantic Ecstasy and Romantic Agony in full measures. There is hardly a romance experience imaginable that is not afforded to her, and thus she is made to discover the falsity of her culture's promises. Norris rubs her nose in the fact that, as Daudet indicated, life is *not* a romance, and we might hazard the platitude that she is a better person for it. A final consideration that does not usually reflect to Norris's credit is that the short fiction he produced between 1901 and 1902 is mainly conventional, popular fiction of the kind a commercial writer produces. They are respectable, worthwhile entertainments, but they are in the same category as Richard Harding Davis's and Stephen Crane's commonplace productions.

Frank Norris was a professional American author seeking to engage the marketplace at the turn of the century and experimenting in many voices and types of writing to win both a reputation and the financial means of pursuing the kind of life he preferred. Occasionally, he obtained world-class status in works that transcended the rest of his canon, with masterpieces of Naturalism such as *McTeague*, *Vandover*, and *The Octopus*. *The Pit* was indeed America's best-selling novel of 1903 and the triumphant example of how far Norris had progressed toward his goal of being both a popular author and an insightful commentator on Western culture in the fin de siècle. As the eulogies that appeared upon his death in October 1902 repeatedly stated, America lost one its most promising talents when Norris died from peritonitis resulting from an appendectomy.[3]

Notes and References

Chapter One

1. Reviews of Norris's books referred to in this chapter are reprinted in Joseph R. McElrath, Jr., and Katherine Knight, *Frank Norris: The Critical Reception* (New York: Burt Franklin, 1981). Contemporaneous descriptions of Norris's initial impact are collected in Joseph R. McElrath, Jr., "Frank Norris: Early Posthumous Responses," *American Literary Realism* 12 (1979): 1-76.

2. W. A. Doggett's comment appeared in an unidentified newspaper clipping in the Frank Norris Collection at the Bancroft Library, University of California, Berkeley. Interviews with Charles G. Norris, Jeannette Norris, and others are alluded to in this chapter; they are all in the Franklin Walker Collection, Bancroft Library. Other sources concerning the relationship between Norris's parents are: Edwin H. Miller, "Frank Norris's *The Pit* as Autobiography," *University of Hartford Studies in Literature* 17 (Summer 1985): 18-32; Richard Allan Davison, "Some Light on Gertrude Doggett Norris's 1894 Divorce Suit," *Frank Norris Studies*, no. 6 (Autumn 1988): 3-4; James Stronks, "Frank Norris and the Eighth Grade," *Frank Norris Studies*, no. 7 (Spring 1989): 2-4; Davison, "The Marriage, Divorce and Demise of a Father of Novelists: B. F. Norris," *Frank Norris Studies*, no. 8 (Autumn 1989): 2-5; Stronks, "The Norris Divorce Suit: Another Newspaper Account," *Frank Norris Studies*, no. 8 (Autumn 1989): 8-9; Stronks, "B. F. Norris (Senior) in Probate Court, with New Light on Frank Norris as Son," *Frank Norris Studies*, no. 11 (Spring 1991): 2-4; and Davison, "Gertrude Doggett Norris: Professional Actress, Dramatic Reader and Mother of Novelists," *Quarterly News-Letter* (San Francisco: Book Club of California), forthcoming.

3. This study is repeatedly informed by the sole full-scale biography by Franklin Walker, *Frank Norris: A Biography* (Garden City, N.Y.: Doubleday, Doran, 1932); hereafter cited in text.

4. "The Way of the World," *The Wave* 9 (16 July 1892): 3-4.

5. "Western Types: An Art Student," *The Wave* 15 (16 May 1896): 10.

6. "Student Life in Paris," *Collier's Weekly* 25 (12 May 1900): 33.

7. *The Pit: A Story of Chicago* (New York: Doubleday, Page, 1903), v.

8. "Story-Tellers vs. Novelists," *World's Work* 3 (March 1902): 1894-97.

125

9. *Frank Norris (1870-1902)* (New York: Doubleday, Page, 1914), 2.

10. "Clothes of Steel," *San Francisco Chronicle*, 31 March 1889, 6.

11. "Brunehilde," *Occident* (University of California) 19 (21 November 1890): 110; "Les Enerves de Jumieges," *Occident* 19 (12 December 1890): 135.

12. *Yvernelle: A Legend of Feudal France* (Philadelphia: Lippincott, 1892).

13. Jesse S. Crisler, ed., *Frank Norris: Collected Letters* (San Francisco: Book Club of California, 1986), 24-26; hereafter cited in text as *Letters*.

14. "The Jongleur of Taillebois," *The Wave* 7, Christmas issue [19 December 1891]: 6-9; "The Son of the Sheik," *Argonaut* 28 (1 June 1891): 6; and "Lauth," *Overland Monthly* 21 (March 1893): 241-60.

15. Numbered I-V, the "Way of the World" stories appeared in *Overland Monthly* as follows: 23 (March 1894): 241-46; 23 (May 1894): 502-6; 24 (July 1894): 82-86; 24 (October 1894): 375-79; and 25 (February 1895): 196-201.

16. James D. Hart, ed., *A Novelist in the Making* (Cambridge: Belknap Press of Harvard University Press, 1970), 97-98; 43 other compositions are included. The forty-fifth is in James D. Hart, ed., *A Student Theme by Frank Norris* (San Francisco: Frank Norris Society, 1987), 2-3.

17. Announced in "Personalities and Politics," *The Wave* 14 (2 November 1895): 6; reprinted with other information on Norris appearing in *The Wave* in Joseph R. McElrath, Jr., "Frank Norris: Biographical Data from *The Wave*: 1891-1901," *Frank Norris Studies*, no. 10 (Fall 1990): 1-12.

18. See Jesse S. Crisler, "Norris in South Africa," *Frank Norris Studies*, no. 7 (Spring 1989): 4-7.

19. "A Californian in the City of Cape Town," *San Francisco Chronicle*, 19 January 1896, 19; "From Cape Town to Kimberley Mine," *San Francisco Chronicle*, 26 January 1896, 1; "In the Compound of a Diamond Mine," *San Francisco Chronicle*, 2 February 1896, 10; "In the Veldt of the Transvaal," *San Francisco Chronicle*, 9 February 1896, 1; "The Uprising in the Transvaal," *San Francisco Chronicle*, 9 February 1896, 17; "The Frantic Rush from Johannesburg," *San Francisco Chronicle*, 1 March 1896, 8; "Street Scenes in Johannesburg During the Insurrection of January, 1896," *Harper's Weekly*, 7 March 1896, 233; "A Zulu War Dance," *San Francisco Chronicle*, 15 March 1896, 1; "Rhodes and the Reporters," *The Wave* 15 (11 April 1896): 5; and "A Steamship Voyage with Cecil Rhodes," *San Francisco Chronicle*, 19 April 1896, 15.

20. Norris's signed and unsigned *Wave* writings are identified in Joseph R. McElrath, Jr., *Frank Norris and "The Wave": A Bibliography* (New York: Garland, 1988).

21. For a fuller picture of Norris's instability than that provided by Walker, see Charles L. Crow, "Bruce Porter's Memoir of Frank Norris," *Frank Norris Studies*, no. 3 (Spring 1987): 1-2.

22. "Little Dramas of the Curbstone," *The Wave* 16 (26 June 1897): 9; "The Sailing of the *Excelsior*," *The Wave* 16 (31 July 1897): 7; and "An Opening for Novelists," *The Wave* 16 (22 May 1897): 7.

23. "The Marriage, Divorce and Demise of a Father of Novelists: B. F. Norris," 3.

24. "Metropolitan Noises," *The Wave* 16 (22 May 1897): 9.

25. Two of Burgess's scrapbooks and his diaries in which Norris is several times named are at the Bancroft Library.

26. Those familiar with Norris only as a "grim Naturalist" will find a different personality in the whimsical Sturgis-Leander series appearing in volume 16 of *The Wave:* "A Bicycle Gymkhana," (10 July 1897): 9; "The Opinions of Leander: 'Holds Forth at Length on the Subject of 'Girl,' " (17 July 1897): 7; "The Opinions of Leander: 'Holdeth Forth upon Our Boys and the Ways of Them," (24 July 1897): 7; "The Opinions of Leander: 'Commenteth at Length upon Letters Received," (31 July 1897): 5; "The Opinions of Leander: 'Falleth from Grace and Subsequently from a Springboard," (7 August 1897): 5-6; "Opinions of Leander: Showing the Plausible Mistake of a Misguided Eastern Man," (14 August 1897): 13; and "Opinions of Justin Sturgis," (21 August 1897): 13.

27. *"Happiness by Conquest,"* *The Wave* 16 (11 December 1897): 2.

28. "Judy's Service of Gold Plate," *The Wave* 16 (16 October 1897): 6; "Fantaisie Printaniere," *The Wave* 16 (6 November 1897): 7.

29. "The Strangest Thing," *The Wave* 16 (3 July 1897): 7; "The House with the Blinds," *The Wave* 16 (21 August 1897): 5; and "The Third Circle," *The Wave* 16 (28 August 1897): 5.

30. " 'Boom,' " *The Wave* 16 (7 August 1897): 5; "Shorty Stack, Pugilist," *The Wave* 16 (20 November 1897): 5-6.

31. "The Associated Un-Charities," *The Wave* 16 (30 October 1897): 7.

32. "His Dead Mother's Portrait," *The Wave* 16 (13 November 1897): 8; "The Puppets and the Puppy," *The Wave* 16 (22 May 1897): 5.

33. "Theory and Reality," *The Wave* 15 (2 May 1896): 8; "What Is Our Greatest Piece of Fiction?" *San Francisco Examiner*, 17 January 1897, 30; and "Zola as a Romantic Writer," *The Wave* 15 (27 June 1896): 3.

34. "Zola's *Rome*," *The Wave* 15 (6 June 1896): 8.

35. "A Reversion to Type," *The Wave* 16 (14 August 1897): 5; "A Case for Lombroso," *The Wave* 16 (11 September 1897): 6.

36. Boswell Jr., "Things and People," *The Wave* 16 (6 March 1897): 7, paragraph 1.

37. This volume, which was never published, was described as "now in press" by Eleanor M. Davenport, "Frank Norris," *University of California Magazine* 3 (November 1897): 80-82.

Chapter Two

1. "An Opening," 7.

2. *Moran of the Lady Letty: A Story of Adventure off the California Coast* (New York: Doubleday & McClure, 1898), iii; hereafter cited in text as *M*.

3. "The Question," *The Wave* 16 (19 June 1897): 13.

4. In chapter 5, *The Wave*, 17 (5 February 1898): 6-7; see *Moran*, 112, where the statement was censored to "smells terribly foul."

5. McElrath and Knight, *Critical Reception*, 60-61.

6. While Donald Pizer analyzes *Moran* in terms of the dynamics of a masculine-feminine ethic, he cannot give it a single identification: "This is either a parody of the romantic adventure novel or one of the best examples of its absurdities"(*The Novels of Frank Norris* [Bloomington: Indiana University Press, 1966], 96).

7. "The Drowned Who Do Not Die," *The Wave* 17 (24 September 1898): 9, 12.

8. McElrath and Knight, *Critical Reception*, 18-20.

9. Ibid., 18.

Chapter Three

1. "*Comida*," *Atlantic Monthly* 83 (March, 1899): 343-83; "With Lawton at El Caney," *Century* 58 (June 1899): 304-9.

2. "Twenty-nine Fatal Wounds," San Francisco *Examiner*, 10 October 1893, 12.

3. "A Summer in Arcady," *The Wave* 15 (25 July 1896): 9.

4. *McTeague: A Story of San Francisco* (New York: Doubleday & McClure, 1899), 1; hereafter cited in text as *Mc*.

5. The degree to which Mac's intelligence is limited is made clear in this burlesque that closes the first chapter. Norris early saw not only the tragic but comic potential of his hero; the scene was developed as a comic sketch when Norris was at Harvard. See Norris's composition dated 20 February 1895 in Hart, *A Novelist in the Making*, 85-86.

6. The traditional interpretation of chapter 2 is that Norris is revealing himself an arch-Victorian rather than a seriocomic post-Victorian describing Mac in the grips of an especially prudish morality. Norris's reactions to human sexuality in *Vandover and the Brute* have been interpreted the same way. See, for example, William B. Dillingham, "Frank Norris and the Genteel Tradition," *Tennessee Studies in Language and Literature* 5 (1960): 15-24.

7. " 'Man Proposes.' – No. 2," *The Wave* 15 (30 May 1896): 7.

8. Barbara Hochman, *The Art of Frank Norris, Storyteller* (Columbia: University of Missouri Press, 1988), 61-76.

9. See, for example, John J. Conder, *Naturalism in American Fiction: The Classic Phase* (Lexington: University of Kentucky Press, 1984), 69-85.

Chapter Four

1. Richard Allan Davison, "Charles G. Norris, Kathleen Norris and *Vandover and the Brute*: A New Letter," *Frank Norris Studies*, no. 3 (Spring 1987): 2-4.

2. Given the anti-Victorian character of *Vandover*, it may be appropriate to recall the beginning of Charles Dickens's portrait of a Victorian moral hero in *David Copperfield*. Unlike the debauched and debilitated Vandover, David narrates his own very lengthy life story with encyclopedic detail and brilliant coherence. It is the first of many ways in which *Vandover* appears *David Copperfield* turned inside out and thus Norris's parody of it.

3. *Vandover and the Brute* (New York: Doubleday, Page, 1914), 3; hereafter cited in text as *V*.

4. The tradition was, once, to see Norris as the arch-Victorian chastising Van for his sins via direct commentary throughout the novel; see, for example, Warren French, *Frank Norris* (New York: Twayne, 1962), 52-61. More recently, the practice has been to differentiate Norris's descriptions and speculations from moments in the narrative in which Norris is expressing *Van's* point of view instead, via free indirect discourse. See Barbara Hochman's summary of such commentary in *The Art of Frank Norris, Storyteller*, 2-3.

5. An ironic tension exists between Van's interpretations of his experience and those to which Norris prompts the reader – as is also the case in *McTeague* with Mac's, Trina's, and Marcus's "readings" of what is transpiring in their lives.

6. Norris thus provides a variation on the theme of enlightenment in Stephen Crane's "The Open Boat," where the shipwreck survivors "felt that they could . . . be interpreters" of the "great sea's voice." Norris makes clear his familiarity with "The Open Boat" in "Perverted Tales," *The Wave*, 16, Christmas issue [18 December 1897], 5-7.

7. In *The Pit*, Norris associates Laura Dearborn with act 3 of this opera, where Gounod's heroine models the ecstasy in love that Laura desires. In *Vandover*, the focus is on act 5 where the sinful heroine is saved from hell because of her contrition. The opera's concept – that it is never too late to be saved from sin – is, apparently, a source of Van's motivation to turn to goodness.

8. For a different perspective on the way in which instinct is a central concept in Norris's thought and art, see William B. Dillingham, *Frank Norris: Instinct and Art* (Lincoln: University of Nebraska Press, 1969).

Chapter Five

1. See the description of the nineteenth-century notion of the ideal woman as man's redeemer in Pizer, *The Novels of Frank Norris*, 86-112.

2. *Blix* (New York: Doubleday & McClure, 1899), 7; hereafter cited in text as *B*.

3. Norris positively employs the departure from Eden image in Genesis once more, in the last chapter of *The Pit*.

4. "The End of the Beginning," *The Wave* 16 (4 September 1897): 5.

5. "The Evolution of a Nurse," *The Wave* 15 (17 October 1896): 8.

6. *A Man's Woman* (New York: Doubleday & McClure, 1900), 2; hereafter cited in text as *W*. While the title page specifies Doubleday & McClure, the actual publisher was the new firm of Doubleday, Page, which employed Norris in January 1900.

Chapter Six

1. While Norris died before the muckraking movement defined itself, he was viewed by its representatives as an early spokesman. See Christopher Wilson, *The Labor of Words: Literary Professionalism in the Progressive Era* (Athens: University of Georgia Press, 1985).

2. In 1901, reviewer Wallace Rice protested that if Norris had intended to expose the "infinitely corrupt corporation methods," *The Octopus* is self-defeated instantly. He could not understand which position – approving or disapproving – Norris had established in the "misshapen" novel (see McElrath and Knight, *Critical Reception*, 124-26). Marxist Granville Hicks, wishing for a wholesale denunciation of laissez-faire capitalism, lamented, "How many problems Norris leaves unsolved" (in *The Great Tradition* [New York: Macmillan, 1933], 171-73). Warren French reflects on how the "book is easily misread . . . because Norris' writing about ideas is often muddy, and it is not easy to distinguish between what he thinks and what his characters think" (*Frank Norris*, 95). For a representative collection of writings on *The Octopus*, see Richard Allan Davison, ed., *The Merrill Studies in* The Octopus (Columbus, Ohio: Charles E. Merrill, 1969).

3. See French's *Frank Norris* regarding Norris as a Transcendentalist. See Pizer's *The Novels of Frank Norris* for an even more influential description of Norris as an optimistic evolutionary idealist and disciple of the evolutionary theist Joseph LeConte.

4. Norris explained in a letter that the "novelist – by nature – can hardly be a political economist; and it is to the latter rather than to the former that one must look for a way out of the 'present discontents'" (*Letters*, 157-59).

5. "Zola as a Romantic Writer," 3.

6. *The Octopus: A Story of California* (New York: Doubleday, Page, 1901), 528; hereafter cited in text as *O*.

7. The scene at Hooven's is mentioned but not given attention by Ronald E. Martin, *American Literature and the Universe of Force* (Durham, N.C.: Duke University Press, 1981), 147-83. Rather, Martin follows tradition by emphasizing Shelgrim's "hard Darwinism" perspective, later synthesized with Vanamee's cosmic optimism, as essential regarding the theme of *The Octopus*.

8. See, for example, Richard Allan Davison, "Frank Norris's *The Octopus*: Some Observations on Vanamee, Shelgrim and St. Paul," *Literature and Ideas in America*, ed. Robert Falk (Athens: University of Ohio Press, 1976), 182-203.

9. See, for example, George H. Sargent's unsigned review reprinted in McElrath and Knight, *Critical Reception*, 157-59.

10. See French, *Frank Norris*, 89-106, and Pizer, *The Novels of Frank Norris*, 113-80.

11. The ongoing debate over *The Octopus* is marked by two extremes: that Norris was incapable of ironic detachment and that Presley's final thoughts are "a double-voiced peroration, the last word of both Presley and

the narrator" (Martin, *Universe of Force,* 171); June Howard focuses not on two voices but one *(Form and History in American Literary Naturalism* [Chapel Hill: University of North Carolina Press, 1985], 123-26).

12. Norris's attitudes toward the type represented by Presley are given a full autobiographical contextualization in Don Graham, *The Fiction of Frank Norris: The Aesthetic Context* (Columbia: University of Missouri Press, 1978), 66-122. Graham, however, sees Presley qua philosopher as expressing a "cosmic optimism" that is the "earned and prepared-for conclusion" to *The Octopus.*

13. We suspect that Norris was indebted to Hamlin Garland. A benevolent character who extends a helping hand to the distressed more succinctly expresses a similar "religion" in "Under the Lion's Paw," which appeared in *Main-Travelled Roads* (1891).

14. "Miracle Joyeux," *The Wave* 16 (9 October 1897): 4. The sentimental Christmas story with which most readers are familiar – *The Joyous Miracle* (New York: Doubleday, Page, 1906) – was a radical revision of the decadent representation of Jesus in the original version.

15. "Literature in the East," *American Art and Literary Review* (Chicago *American*), 25 May 1901, 8, 12; "Frank Norris' Weekly Letter" articles appeared in 1901 from 1 June to 15 June on p. 5, from 22 June to 20 July on p. 8, from 3 August to 10 August on p. 5, and from 24 August to 31 August on p. 8. No "Letter" was published on 27 July 1901.

16. *The Responsibilities of the Novelist and Other Literary Essays* (New York: Doubleday, Page, 1903).

17. "The Riding of Felipe," *Everybody's Magazine* 4 (March 1901): 254-66; "Buldy Jones, *Chef de Claque,*" *Everybody's Magazine* 4 (May 1901): 449-59; and "A Plea for Romantic Fiction," *Boston Evening Transcript,* 8 January 1901, 14.

Chapter Seven

1. *The Pit: A Story of Chicago* (New York: Doubleday, Page, 1903), 20; hereafter cited in text as *P.*

2. This aria closes act 3 of the opera, and it precipitates the ecstatic climax of Faust's courtship. As Marguerite sings, Faust's arousal peaks. The curtain falls as he rushes to her and they embrace. The degree to which Norris was indebted to Gustave Flaubert may be seen in a comparison of chapter 1 of *The Pit* with the description of Emma at the opera in *Madame Bovary,* part 2, chapter 15.

3. For another fictional exposé of the kind by Norris, see "A Deal in Wheat," *Everybody's Magazine* 7 (August 1902): 173-80. See also "Life in

the Mining Region," *Everybody's Magazine* 7 (September 1902): 241-48, wherein Norris again effects a more "balanced" picture of the relationship between "capital" and "labor" like that attempted in *The Octopus*. While "A Deal in Wheat" invites a left-wing interpretation of Norris, the latter clarifies his dominant, middle-of-the-road attitude.

4. "The Pit," *Saturday Evening Post*, 175 (15 November 1902): 10. The serialization ran from 20 September 1902 through 31 January 1903.

5. That the husband and wife are thus separated, with their experiences standing as individuated rather than shared, has resulted in negative criticism of the novel's structure. Laura's story and Curtis's are seen as self-contained to the degree that *The Pit* does not seem an integrated whole. See, for example, James D. Hart's Introduction to *The Pit* (Columbus, Ohio: Charles E. Merrill, 1970), xii-xiii.

6. See *The Pit*, 244-47. Norris satirically develops the discussion of evolutionary philosophy between Corthell and Laura. Corthell – intent on seduction – articulates an optimistic view of the development of the human race that minimizes the significance of the individual and, thus, the moral responsibility of the individual. It positions him nicely to encourage Laura's guilt-free descent into adultery. Laura unsophisticatedly accepts Corthell's pink-horizoned vista, coming to the pleasant conclusion that God is effecting evolutionary progress, with or without the cooperation of the individual. The scene appears a companion piece for the conclusion of *The Octopus*. For another point of view on the scene, see Pizer's *The Novels of Frank Norris*, 175: Pizer evaluates it as Norris's ineffectual attempt to develop seriously, rather than satirically, a theme concerning the "universal benevolence of racial evolution."

7. We may recall the death scene at Hooven's house in *The Octopus* when, once, the villain of that novel, S. Behrman, emerges from self-absorption to show concern for another.

Conclusion

1. Donald Pizer, "Late Nineteenth-Century American Naturalism," *Realism and Naturalism in Nineteenth-Century American Literature*, rev. ed. (Carbondale: Southern Illinois University Press, 1984), 9-30.

2. See Joseph R. McElrath, Jr., "The Comedy of Frank Norris's *McTeague*," *Studies in American Humor* 2 (1975): 88-95, and his Introduction to *Critical Reception*, xiv. Norris's more serious uses of comic devices are considered in James E. Caron, "Grotesque Naturalism: The Significance of the Comic in *McTeague*," *Texas Studies in Literature and Language*, 31 (1989): 288-317.

3. See McElrath, "Frank Norris: Early Posthumous Responses."

Selected Bibliography

Listed are the most authoritative individual editions of Frank Norris's book-length works and collections of shorter writings. Most are available in photo-offset, facsimile printings listed in *Books in Print*. The several collected editions of Norris's writings published after 1902 are not textually reliable, and there is no complete collection of the works. The fullest immediately accessible collected edition is the 1928 *Argonaut Manuscript Limited Edition*, reprinted as *Complete Edition* in 1929. The 1983-84 *Works of Frank Norris* is more complete but difficult to locate outside Japan. See *Frank Norris: A Descriptive Bibliography*, below, for a complete record of Norris's publications and the books and periodicals in which they may be found.

PRIMARY WORKS

Poetry

Yvernelle: A Legend of Feudal France. Philadelphia: J. B. Lippincott, 1892.

Novels

Moran of the Lady Letty: A Story of Adventure off the California Coast. New York: Doubleday & McClure, 1898.

McTeague: A Story of San Francisco. New York: Doubleday & McClure, 1899.

Blix. New York: Doubleday & McClure, 1899.

A Man's Woman. New York: Doubleday & McClure, 1900.

The Octopus: A Story of California. New York: Doubleday, Page, 1901.

The Pit: A Story of Chicago. New York: Doubleday, Page, 1903.

Vandover and the Brute. Garden City, New York: Doubleday, Page, 1914.

Short Stories, Essays, Articles, and Reviews

A Deal in Wheat and Other Stories of the New and Old West. New York: Doubleday, Page, 1903.

The Responsibilities of the Novelist and Other Literary Essays. New York: Doubleday, Page, 1903.

The Joyous Miracle. New York: Doubleday, Page, 1906.

The Third Circle. New York: John Lane, 1909.

The Surrender of Santiago. San Francisco: Paul Elder, 1917.

Frank Norris of "The Wave." Edited by Oscar Lewis. San Francisco: Westgate Press, 1931.

The Literary Criticism of Frank Norris. Edited by Donald Pizer. Austin: University of Texas Press, 1964.

A Novelist in the Making: A Collection of the Student Themes and the Novels "Blix" and "Vandover and the Brute." Edited by James D. Hart. Cambridge: The Belknap Press of Harvard University Press, 1970.

A Student Theme by Frank Norris. Ed. James D. Hart. Berkeley, Calif.: Frank Norris Society, 1987.

Collected Editions

Complete Works of Frank Norris. 7 vols. New York: Doubleday, Page, 1903.

The Complete Works of Frank Norris. 4 vols. New York: P. F. Collier, 1905.

The Argonaut Manuscript Limited Edition. 10 vols. Garden City, New York: Doubleday, Doran, 1928; also published as *Complete Edition*, 1928.

The Works of Frank Norris. 12 vols. Edited by Kenji Inoue. Tokyo: Meicho Fukyu Kai, 1983-84.

Letters

Frank Norris: Collected Letters. Edited by Jesse S. Crisler. San Francisco: Book Club of California, 1986.

SECONDARY WORKS

Primary Bibliographies

McElrath, Joseph R., Jr. *Frank Norris: A Descriptive Bibliography*. Pittsburgh: University of Pittsburgh Press, 1992.

_____. *Frank Norris and "The Wave": A Bibliography*. New York: Garland, 1988.

Secondary Bibliographies

Crisler, Jesse S., and Joseph R. McElrath, Jr. *Frank Norris: A Reference Guide*. Boston: G. K. Hall, 1974.

Dean, Thomas K., and others. "Current Publications." *Frank Norris Studies*, no. 2 (Autumn 1986), and subsequent issues.

Dillingham, William B. "Frank Norris." In *Fifteen American Authors before 1900*, rev. ed., edited by Earl N. Harbert and Robert E. Rees, pp. 402-38. Madison: University of Wisconsin Press, 1984.

Biographies

Norris, Charles G. *Frank Norris (1870-1902)*. Garden City, N.Y.: Doubleday, Page, 1914.

Poncet, André. *Frank Norris (1870-1902)*. 2 vols. Paris: Librairie Honoré Champion, 1977.

Walker, Franklin. *Frank Norris: A Biography*. Garden City, N.Y.: Doubleday, Doran, 1932.

Criticism: Books

Ahnebrink, Lars. *The Influence of Emile Zola on Frank Norris*. Cambridge: Harvard University Press, 1947.

Davison, Richard Allan, comp. *The Merrill Studies in "The Octopus."* Columbus, Ohio: Charles E. Merrill, 1969. Collection of representative interpretations of *The Octopus*, letters by Norris concerning it, and reviews.

Dillingham, William B. *Frank Norris: Instinct and Art*. Lincoln: University of Nebraska Press, 1969. Focuses on Norris's personality and works, identifying themes dealing with masculinity, instinct, and the "darker" aspects of human experience. Analyzes his theory and practice in regard to style.

French, Warren. *Frank Norris*. New York: Twayne Publishers, 1962. A biographical and critical study.

Frohock, W. M. *Frank Norris*. Minneapolis: University of Minnesota Press, 1969. Depicts Norris as a Zola disciple who made melodramatic use of Naturalistic literary techniques.

Graham, Don. *The Fiction of Frank Norris: The Aesthetic Context*. Columbia: University of Missouri Press, 1978. Analyzes Norris's highly allusive art, explaining how cultural-contextual references are essential to characterization and theme.

_____, comp. *Critical Essays on Frank Norris*. Boston: G. K. Hall, 1980. Collects reviews of Norris's novels and interpretations of Norris's life and works.

Hochman, Barbara. *The Art of Frank Norris, Storyteller*. Columbia: University of Missouri Press, 1988. Eschews conventional interpretations of Norris's fiction as Naturalistic and examines the novels in terms of their foci on the "vulnerability of the self."

McElrath, Joseph R., Jr., and Katherine Knight, comps. *Frank Norris: The Critical Reception*. New York: Burt Franklin, 1981. Collects the reviews of Norris's works identified through 1980.

Marchand, Ernest. *Frank Norris: A Study*. Palo Alto, Calif.: Stanford University Press, 1942. Comprehensive analysis of Norris's thought and works.

Pizer, Donald. *The Novels of Frank Norris*. Bloomington: Indiana University Press, 1966. Interprets Norris's novels in the context of Joseph LeConte's ethical evolutionary idealism.

Criticism: Parts of Books

Ahnebrink, Lars. *The Beginnings of Naturalism in American Fiction*. Cambridge: Harvard University Press, 1950. Expansion of *The Influence of Emile Zola on Frank Norris*, above, differentiating Norris's Naturalism from that seen in the writings of other Americans.

Borus, Daniel H. *Writing Realism: Howells, James, and Norris in the Mass Market*. Chapel Hill: University of North Carolina Press, 1989. Examines the techniques employed by Realist writers in light of the nature of their readership and the historical circumstances; examines Norris's methodology and his view of the social role of an author.

Chase, Richard. *The American Novel and Its Tradition*. Garden City, N.Y.: Doubleday, 1957. Focuses on the characteristics of the American romance-novel, describing *McTeague* and *The Octopus* in terms of their Romantic characteristics.

Conder, John J. *Naturalism in American Fiction: The Classic Phase*. Lexington: University of Kentucky Press, 1984. Analyzes Norris as an author rigidly applying a deterministic philosophy in *McTeague*.

Davison, Richard Allan. *Charles G. Norris*. Boston: Twayne, 1983. A biographical and critical study of Frank Norris's brother; includes essential information on the Norris family and Frank's influence on Charles.

Gardner, Joseph. *Dickens in America: Twain, Howells, James, and Norris*. New York: Garland, 1988. Examines the apparent influences of Dickens's works on Norris's.

Howard, June. *Form and History in American Literary Naturalism*. Chapel Hill: University of North Carolina Press, 1985. Identifies salient characteristics of Naturalistic fiction; focuses on *McTeague, Vandover*, and *The Octopus*.

Martin, Jay. *Harvests of Change: American Literature, 1865-1914*. Englewood Cliffs, N.J.: Prentice-Hall, 1967. Describes the preoccupations and accomplishments of American writers in the post–Civil War period, portraying Norris and others in their ambitious attempts to address national experience in a Great American Novel.

Martin, Ronald E. *American Literature and the Universe of Force*. Durham, N.C.: Duke University Press, 1981. Pictures Norris as an absolutist thinker in his optimistic description of how natural forces determine the character of life.

Marx, Leo. *The Machine in the Garden: Technology and the Pastoral Idea in America*. New York: Oxford University Press, 1967. Explains the literary consequences of the rural-agrarian character of the United States being displaced by a technological-industrial order, finding in *The Octopus* dramatic imagery indicating the dominance of the "machine."

Michaels, Walter Benn. *The Gold Standard and the Logic of Naturalism: American Literature at the Turn of the Century*. Berkeley: University of California Press, 1987. Interprets Norris's and other Naturalistic works in light of economic conditions and concepts related to them at the close of the nineteenth century.

Mitchell, Lee Clark. *Determined Fictions: American Literary Naturalism*. New York: Columbia University Press, 1989. Analyzes the style of Naturalistic works and how it reflects the vision of the author; focuses on *Vandover* in terms of how Van's way of thinking of his experience constitutes a psychological determinism.

Pizer, Donald. *Realism and Naturalism in Late Nineteenth-Century American Literature*. Rev. ed. Carbondale: Southern Illinois University Press, 1984. Collection of essays by Pizer; "Late Nineteenth Century American Naturalism" defines Naturalistic fiction as embodying Humanistic concerns, rather than just a "pessimistic materialistic determinism"; other topics addressed include Norris's definition of Naturalism, the significance of Norris's literary criticism, and Marx's misreading of *The Octopus* in *The Machine in the Garden*.

Ziff, Larzer. *The American 1890s: Life and Times of a Lost Generation*. New York: Viking, 1966. Explains Norris as a progressive writer attempting to examine and express a modern point of view appropriate for the late nineteenth century.

Index

141

The Author

Joseph R. McElrath, Jr., is professor of English at Florida State University, where he has taught since 1974. He earned his B.A. at LeMoyne College, his M.A. at Duquesne University, and his Ph.D. at the University of South Carolina. He is the co-author of *Frank Norris: A Reference Guide* (1974) and *Frank Norris: The Critical Reception* (1981) and author of *Frank Norris and "The Wave": A Bibliography* (1988) and *Frank Norris: A Descriptive Bibliography* (1992). He has served on the Board of Directors of The Frank Norris Society since 1985 and is editor in chief of the in-progress (10-volume) *Centennial Edition of the Writings of Frank Norris.*